Goldendoodles as Pets

The Ultimate Goldendoodle Owner's Guide

Goldendoodle Breeding, Where to Buy, Types, Care, Cost, Diet, Grooming, and Training all Included.

By: Lolly Brown

Copyrights and Trademarks

All rights reserved. No part of this book may be reproduced or transformed in any form or by any means, graphic, electronic, or mechanical, including photocopying, recording, taping, or by any information storage retrieval system, without the written permission of the author.

This publication is Copyright ©2016. All products, graphics, publications, software and services mentioned and recommended in this publication are protected by trademarks. In such instance, all trademarks & copyright belong to the respective owners.

Disclaimer and Legal Notice

This product is not legal, medical, or accounting advice and should not be interpreted in that manner. You need to do your own due-diligence to determine if the content of this product is right for you. While every attempt has been made to verify the information shared in this publication, neither the author, neither publisher, nor the affiliates assume any responsibility for errors, omissions or contrary interpretation of the subject matter herein. Any perceived slights to any specific person(s) or organization(s) are purely unintentional.

We have no control over the nature, content and availability of the web sites listed in this book. The inclusion of any web site links does not necessarily imply a recommendation or endorse the views expressed within them. We take no responsibility for, and will not be liable for, the websites being temporarily unavailable or being removed from the internet.

The accuracy and completeness of information provided herein and opinions stated herein are not guaranteed or warranted to produce any particular results, and the advice and strategies, contained herein may not be suitable for every individual. Neither the author nor the publisher shall be liable for any loss incurred as a consequence of the use and application, directly or indirectly, of any information presented in this work. This publication is designed to provide information in regard to the subject matter covered.

Neither the author nor the publisher assume any responsibility for any errors or omissions, nor do they represent or warrant that the ideas, information, actions, plans, suggestions contained in this book is in all cases accurate. It is the reader's responsibility to find advice before putting anything written in this book into practice. The information in this book is not intended to serve as legal, medical, or accounting advice.

Foreword

The Goldendoodle is just one of many designer dogs that have recently gained popularity. Some have called this nothing more than a fad, others have fallen quite in love with their designer dogs. Goldendoodles do rank quite highly among people's regard compared to other designer dog crossbreeds. With the temperament of a Golden Retriever, and the beautiful coat of a Poodle, this cross is a very easy dog to love.

If you have been considering getting a Goldendoodle for a pet, it is best to find out all you can about the breed's unique quirks and traits before you bring one home. This is a sociable, well-adjusted animal that does can be a little demanding in terms of grooming.

And like most designer dogs, they can be a little pricey, but given the unique combination of the best traits of two purebreds, this can be a worthwhile investment in a loving and loyal companion.

Table of Contents

Introduction 1
    Glossary of Dog Terms 2
Chapter One: Understanding Goldendoodles 9
    Facts About Goldendoodles 10
    Summary of Goldendoodle Facts 12
    Goldendoodle Breed History 14
Chapter Two: Things to Know Before Getting a Goldendoodle 17
    Do You Need a License? 18
    How Many Goldendoodles Should You Keep? 19
    Do Goldendoodles Get Along with Other Pets? 20
    How Much Does it Cost to Keep a Goldendoodle? 21
    What are the Pros and Cons of Goldendoodles? 24
        Pros for the Goldendoodle Breed 24
        Cons for the Goldendoodle Breed 25
Chapter Three: Purchasing Your Goldendoodle 27
    Where Can You Buy a Goldendoodle? 28
    How to Choose a Reputable Goldendoodle Breeder ... 29
    Tips for Selecting a Healthy Goldendoodle Puppy 32
    Puppy-Proofing Your Home 35
Chapter Four: Caring for Your New Goldendoodle 39

Ideal Habitat Requirements for Goldendoodles 40

Supplies and Equipment to Have on Hand 41

Exercise Requirements for the Goldendoodle 43

Chapter Five: Meeting Your Goldendoodle's Nutritional Needs 45

    The Nutritional Needs of Dogs 46

        Proteins 47

        Carbohydrates 47

        Fats 48

        Vitamins and Minerals 48

    Daily Energy Requirements 48

    How to Select a Quality Dog Food Brand 51

    Dangerous Foods to Avoid 54

Chapter Six: Training Your Goldendoodle 57

    Socializing Your New Goldendoodle Puppy 59

    Housebreaking your Goldendoodle Puppy 61

    Positive Reinforcement for Obedience Training 64

Chapter Seven: Grooming Your Goldendoodle 67

    Recommended Tools to Have on Hand 69

    Tips for Bathing Goldendoodles 70

    Tips for Grooming Your Goldendoodle 71

    Other Grooming Tasks 72

Brushing Your Goldendoodle's Teeth 72

Trimming Your Goldendoodle's Nails 74

Cleaning Your Goldendoodle's Ears 75

Chapter Eight: Breeding Your Goldendoodle 77

Breeding Goldendoodles and Designer Dogs 78

Basic Dog Breeding Information 82

Tips for Caring for your Pregnant Goldendoodle 84

Whelping Goldendoodle Puppies 87

Caring for and Weaning the Puppies 89

Chapter Nine: Keeping Your Goldendoodle Healthy 93

Common Health Problems Affecting Goldendoodles 96

    Hip Dysplasia 97

    Elbow Dysplasia 99

    Hypothyroidism 101

    Von Willebrand's Disease 103

    Eye Conditions 104

    Patellar Luxation 110

    Sebacious Adenitis 111

    Ear Infections 112

    Allergies 113

    Gastric Dilatation-Volvulus 114

Preventing Illness with Vaccinations 115

Goldendoodle Care Sheet 119
   1.) Basic Goldendoodle Information 120
   2.) Habitat Requirements 122
   3.) Nutritional Needs 123
   4.) Breeding Information 124
Index 127
Photo Credits 135
References 137

Introduction

Goldendoodles are a recent crossbreed hybrid, the result of a mix between a Golden Retriever and a Poodle. Because this is a fairly recent crossbreed, there is much variation still in Goldendoodle types, and they can range in size from large, standard, or miniature. Their coat types can also range from wavy, to fleece, to curly, depending on which gene pool is more dominant.

Interestingly, compared to most designer breeds, the temperament of Goldendoodles is fairly consistent. This is a sweet, gentle and affectionate dog that is quite intelligent

Introduction

and easy to train. They make great family pets, though not effective guard dogs since they are more likely to wag their tails at strangers than to bark. They are wonderful for first time dog owners, and are quite adaptable in living situations, thriving just as well in an apartment as in a rural farm. As long as you make sure they have regular exercise, a good and nutritious diet, and constant love and affection, this can be a perfect breed for you.

Glossary of Dog Terms

AKC – American Kennel Club, the largest purebred dog registry in the United States

Almond Eye – Referring to an elongated eye shape rather than a rounded shape

Balance – A show term referring to all of the parts of the dog, both moving and standing, which produce a harmonious image

Beard – Long, thick hair on the dog's underjaw

Best in Show – An award given to the only undefeated dog left standing at the end of judging

Bitch – A female dog

Introduction

Bite – The position of the upper and lower teeth when the dog's jaws are closed; positions include level, undershot, scissors, or overshot

Board – To house, feed, and care for a dog for a fee

Break - When the puppy's coat color changes as an adult

Breed – A domestic race of dogs having a common gene pool and characterized appearance/function

Breed Standard – A published document describing the look, movement, and behavior of the perfect specimen of a particular breed

Buff – An off-white to gold coloring

Castrate - The removal of the testicles of a male dog.

Character - The individuality, general appearance, expression and deportment considered typical of a breed.

Clip – A method of trimming the coat in some breeds

Coarse - Lacks refinement.

Coat – The hair covering of a dog; some breeds have two coats, and outer coat and undercoat; also known as a double coat. Examples of breeds with double coats include German Shepherd, Siberian Husky, Akita, etc.

Condition – The health of the dog as shown by its skin, coat, behavior, and general appearance

Introduction

Conformation - Form and structure of shape and parts in conformance with breed standards

Crate – A container used to house and transport dogs; also called a cage or kennel

Crossbreed (Hybrid) – A dog having a sire and dam of two different breeds; cannot be registered with the AKC

Dam (bitch) – The female parent of a dog;

Dominance - Displays of assertiveness of one dog over other dogs

Double Coat – Having an outer weather-resistant coat and a soft, waterproof coat for warmth; see above.

Ear set - A description of where the ears are set on the head

Even bite - Also *level bite,* meeting of upper and lower incisors without any overlapping

Ear leather - The flap of the ear

Feathering – A long fringe of hair on the ears, tail, legs, or body of a dog

Fetch - A game of retrieval

Gait - A pattern of steps with a particular rhythm and footfall

Game - Wild animals being hunted

Introduction

Genealogy - Also *Pedigree*.

Gestation Period - From the time of mating until birth.

Gun dog - Dog trained to hunt game.

Groom – To brush, trim, comb or otherwise make a dog's coat neat in appearance

Heat - Estrus, fertile period of the female.

Heel – To command a dog to stay close by its owner's side

Hip Dysplasia – A condition characterized by the abnormal formation of the hip joint

Inbreeding – The breeding of two closely related dogs of one breed

Interbreeding - The breeding of dogs of different breeds

Kennel – A building or enclosure where dogs are kept

Lead - Leash

Litter – A group of puppies born at one time

Markings – A contrasting color or pattern on a dog's coat

Mate – To breed a dog and a bitch

Milk teeth - Baby teeth

Mongrel - The result of crossbreeding

Neuter – To castrate a male dog or spay a female dog

Introduction

Pads – The tough, shock-absorbent skin on the bottom of a dog's foot

Pedigree – The written record of a dog's genealogy going back three generations or more

Point - A stylized stance of a hunting dog to indicate the location of game

Puppy – A dog under 12 months of age

Purebred – A dog whose sire and dam belong to the same breed and who are of unmixed descent

Retrieve - Bringing back game to the hunter

Retrieving Breeds - Sporting breeds that retrieve birds from water or over land

Shedding – The natural process whereby old hair falls off the dog's body as it is replaced by new hair growth.

Sire – The male parent of a dog

Smooth Coat – Short hair that is close-lying

Spay – The surgery to remove a female dog's ovaries, rendering her incapable of breeding

Stud - Male dog used for breeding

Tricolor - a coat of three distinct colors, usually black, white and tan

Introduction

Trim – To groom a dog's coat by plucking or clipping

Type - A sum of qualities distinguishing a specific breed or a specific dog

Undercoat – The soft, short coat typically concealed by a longer outer coat

Wean – The process through which puppies transition from subsisting on their mother's milk to eating solid food

Whelping – The act of birthing a litter of puppies

Whiskers - Sensory organs consisting of hairs on the sides of a dog's muzzle

Introduction

Chapter One: Understanding Goldendoodles

If you are considering bringing a Goldendoodle into your home, it is always a good idea to learn more about the breed's unique quirks, traits, and characteristics. This will enable you to judge beforehand whether or not you and a dog will be a good "fit." After all, if the regular grooming and maintenance needs of a Goldendoodle is, for instance,

Chapter One: Understanding Goldendoodles

something that you cannot reasonably provide, then perhaps this is not the breed for you, and you should turn your sights to a dog breed that is a little more low maintenance.

Also knowing about the Goldendoodle's needs will allow you to evaluate your home, surroundings and lifestyle to determine whether or your home is a place where this dog hybrid can thrive. Of course, being a relatively new breed, there is still a certain amount of uncertainty and unpredictability when it comes to Goldendoodles. Compared to many other recent designer crossbreeds, however, Goldendoodles are comparatively predictable when it comes to their temperament, grooming, exercise, and nutritional needs.

Let us begin our acquaintance with the Goldendoodle with a brief overview and summary of the interesting facts about this very popular crossbreed.

Facts About Goldendoodles

Goldendoodles are a crossbreed mix of two purebred dogs: the Golden Retriever and the Poodle. It is one of many recent crossbreeding attempts to produce what are more popularly known as "designer dogs." Designer dogs are usually recognized by their unique names: a mash-up of the names of the two purebreds that have been crossed,

Chapter One: Understanding Goldendoodles

resulting in a cutesy kind of name that perfectly fits the small and cute crossbreed puppies.

Crossbreeding dogs is an old practice - and many of the purebreds we know and love today were also the result of crossbreeding attempts of people years ago. It was, and is still, an endeavor at isolating desirable traits that may be characteristic of two or more different breeds, and brought together in a hybrid mix that carries these desired traits. When once before people crossbred dogs for functional purposes such as hunting and retrieving functions, the crossbreeding of designer dogs were designed to bring together function, coat characteristics, and a size amenable to city living.

The original designer dog was a Poodle and Labrador Retriever mix that was intended to serve as a guide dog while at the same time have a hypoallergenic coat for those people who also suffered from allergies. The intent behind the crossbreeding of Golden Retrievers and Poodles is much the same. While this breed's traits are not yet firmly established - there is still a wide variety among Goldendoodles in terms of their size and their coat types, breeding attempts are still continuing to isolate the ideal: temperamentally similar to a Golden Retriever but with a hypo-allergenic coat similar to a Poodle. More recently, miniature Poodles were also used as a cross to produce smaller sized Goldendoodles who would be perfect dogs for people living in apartments.

Chapter One: Understanding Goldendoodles

Much criticism has been leveled against the fad of "designer dogs" because this has produced crossbreeds with lots of inherited sicknesses. But this is mainly due to the proliferation of puppy mills who only want to cash in on the designer dog fad, and are breeding dogs purely for profit. Provided there is responsible breeding, there is no reason at all why Goldendoodles should not be reasonably healthy and hardy, and they can, in fact, live for as long as 15 years.

Regardless of which side of the crossbreeding fad you are on, one really cannot deny the unique charm and appeal of Goldendoodles, and how quickly they have made their way into people's hearts. This is a very loveable and affectionate breed, intelligent, well-trained, loyal, and family friendly. It is a perfect dog for first time owners, and the miniature Goldendoodles can fit nicely in an apartment. There are also many breeders out there who are fully committed to the future and welfare of this crossbreed, and who breed responsibly for the betterment of the breed. Who knows, maybe in a few more years, Goldendoodles might even achieve official recognition and purebred status?

Summary of Goldendoodle Facts

Pedigree: Golden Retriever, Poodle

Chapter One: Understanding Goldendoodles

AKC Group: not applicable; this is a relatively new breed that is not yet recognized by any of the international dog organizations

Types: no distinctions as to type

Breed Size: can range from standard, medium, and miniature

Height: for Standard Goldendoodles, height is at 22-26 inches tall at the withers; mini Goldendoodles have an average height of from 10-15 inches tall at the withers

Weight: Standard Goldendoodles can weigh from 50 to 90 lbs.; mini Goldendoodles weigh from 10 to 30 lbs

Coat: can be either wavy or curly, and may be (but not always) hypoallergenic and non-shedding; coats can resemble either of their parents' coats

Coat Color: variety of colors, including apricot, red, gold, black, silver, blue, chocolate, fawn, white, or parti-colored

Eyes: eyes are almond-shaped and can range in colors from brown, green, blue and amber;

Ears: can vary from long, heavy hanging ears or shorter ears that flip over the top

Temperament: friendly, loving, gentle, playful, trusting, naturally intelligent and biddable, and eager to please

Chapter One: Understanding Goldendoodles

Strangers: are friendly with strangers, do not make good guard dogs; toy Goldendoodles may not be stranger-friendly

Other Dogs: provided proper introduction and socialization, generally get along well with other dogs

Other Pets: provided proper introduction and socialization, get along well with other pets

Training: highly intelligent and easy to train; responds well to positive reinforcement

Exercise Needs: regular, moderate exercise and periods of play

Health Conditions: Hip Dysplasia, Elbow Dysplasia, Hypothyroidism, Von Willebrand's Disease, Eye Conditions (such as Juvenile-onset cataracts, Eyelid abnormalities [Entropion/Ectropion], Progressive Retinal Atrophy, and Glaucoma), Patellar Luxation, Sebacious Adenitis, Ear Infections, Allergies, and Gastric Dilatation-Volvulus (Bloat)

Lifespan: average 10 to 13 years

Goldendoodle Breed History

The Goldendoodle's history is recent - a spinoff from the growing popularity of Labradoodles and other designer dogs. Most hybrid/designer dogs usually do involve crossbreeding with a Poodle because of the desirable

Chapter One: Understanding Goldendoodles

hypoallergenic coats, and it really wasn't long before the loveable Golden Retriever was taken in hand and Goldendoodles first saw the light of day. Just as with Labradoodles - the intention was to create a crossbreed that would be suitable guide dogs with low-shedding, hypoallergenic coats that would be a good fit for those who also had allergies.

The first Goldendoodle originated in Australia in the 1980s, and then in North America sometime in the 1990s, while the mini or medium Goldendoodle - the result of a cross between a Golden Retriever and a miniature Poodle - was produced in January 2002. Aside from a wonderful temperament and ideal coat, the Goldendoodle added a size that was also perfect for apartment and city living. Since then, the popularity of this crossbreed has only increased.

The Goldendoodle's name also went through a mini-evolution of sorts: in the beginning, various names were used to describe them such as Groodles, GoldenPoos, GoldiePoos, and even PoodleReivers. It was Goldendoodle that stuck, however, and that is the name that the breed goes by today.

It bears mentioning that not all crossbreed/hybrid offsprings or generations have allergy-friendly coats, and not all may have the desired temperament, either. Breeding attempts do still result in a great variety of characteristics among the offsprings. But while not all Goldendoodles may

Chapter One: Understanding Goldendoodles

have hypo-allergenic coats, or the suitable temperaments to be guide dogs, the popularity of Goldendoodles have made them more than just a passing designer dog fad - and each generation, regardless of which qualities turn out to be dominant, are still hybrid Goldendoodles, and are lovable for what they are.

In general, Goldendoodles are social, energetic and playful by nature, and are very trainable. They have since proven popular as therapy and service dogs, and they certainly make great family pets.

Chapter Two: Things to Know Before Getting a Goldendoodle

After this brief introduction with the Goldendoodle breed, you might be wondering what it actually means to have a Goldendoodle as a pet. In the following chapters, we explore more about what it means to take care of Goldendoodles, including grooming, socialization, nutrition, training, exercise, and their health concerns. All this will give you a better understanding of this new breed, what

Chapter Two: Things to Know Before Getting a Goldendoodle

ideal lifestyle will be feasible for keeping a dog such as a Goldendoodle, and whether or not this is the right breed for you.

As a preliminary, however, this chapter summarizes some of the more practical factors involved in Goldendoodle ownership. We take a closer look at the question of licenses, costs, keeping other pets in addition to a Goldendoodle, and a general overview of the pros and cons of this hybrid crossbreed.

Do You Need a License?

Dog licensing regulations vary depending on your region. There aren't really any federal laws regarding this, as this is more of a local matter. The best way to check whether you will need to secure a license for your dog is to check with your local legislature or council to determine what requirements prevail in your area.

Even if you are not legally required to get a license, however, it might be a good idea to do so voluntarily anyway. This way, your ownership is legally registered, and it will be easier for other people to trace your dog back to you in case he ever gets lost. It will also be a good way to assert your ownership over your Goldendoodle in case such a situation ever arises. If

Licenses in general are only granted after the payment of a small fee, and proof of rabies vaccination.

Chapter Two: Things to Know Before Getting a Goldendoodle

Since you should have your dog vaccinated against rabies anyway, this isn't really a troublesome requirement. Licenses are usually renewable on an annual basis, during which time you should again provide proof of revaccination. This tells us that licensing is intended not only to regulate ownership, but also to protect both your dog and the public against rabies. Again, check your local laws to verify the specific requirements prevailing in your region.

How Many Goldendoodles Should You Keep?

The decision to keep more than one Goldendoodle is a personal one, and each person will have to make this decision based on his or her unique circumstances. Perhaps the only thing that need be said on this score is that you should only keep more than one Goldendoodle if you are sure that you can afford their upkeep, including food, grooming, medical expenses, and also have the time and energy to socialize, exercise, groom and train with both dogs on a regular basis.

As you will see later in this chapter, keeping one dog can easily translate to a substantial yearly cost, and keeping more than one dog will easily translate to at least double this basic amount. And taking care of any dog requires energy commitment that a full time working person may not be able

Chapter Two: Things to Know Before Getting a Goldendoodle

to spare. The main consideration you should have on keeping more than one Goldendoodle is whether or not this is for the best interests of the dog. If doing so will mean that you will not be able to provide fully for each of them, or that it is beyond your financial capacity, then the answer is probably no.

If you can afford it easily, however, without any detrimental effect on your own expenses, and if you have the room, the time and the energy for it, then certainly having more than one Goldendoodle in the house can be a very rewarding and enjoyable experience. This is a very loving, affectionate and intelligent breed, and having more than one to keep you - and each other - company, can be worthwhile.

Do Goldendoodles Get Along with Other Pets?

Goldendoodles are a generally friendly breed. Provided there was proper socialization training in his early months and years, Goldendoodles can be quite popular and well-loved by other pets, by your other family members, by the neighbors, and even by strangers!

Yes, this is a sociable breed, and they are just as likely to wag their tail at strangers coming to your door rather than

Chapter Two: Things to Know Before Getting a Goldendoodle

bark a warning. They will also prove to be loyal and affectionate companions to other pets, whether it be another dog, another Goldendoodle, or even cats! Just make sure that you properly supervise the introductory meetings between your Goldendoodle and other pets.

If you keep other smaller pets, such as birds or mice, for instance, it is probably best to exercise due caution as Goldendoodles do descend from Golden Retrievers - a hunting dog known for chasing small prey.

How Much Does it Cost to Keep a Goldendoodle?

Finally, let's talk numbers. One of the things you'll probably notice during the process of adoption or purchase of a Goldendoodle puppy is a series of questions regarding your lifestyle, your home situation, and your financial situation. This is because breeders and those who work at finding homes for rescues know that the costs of keeping a pet can add up. Aside from various dog equipment and accessories, there is also the annual cost of food, medical expenses, vaccinations, and grooming. All these are necessary for your dog to live a long, healthy and fulfilling life, and any person interested in keeping a Goldendoodle should be able to show that they can afford the yearly costs.

Chapter Two: Things to Know Before Getting a Goldendoodle

How much, do you wonder, does keeping a Goldendoodle cost?

Your expenses will necessarily be larger during the first year, as there will be one-time initial expenses such as the cost of purchase or adoption (the purchase price of a Goldendoodle puppy can range from around $1,400 to as high as $3,000), spaying and/or neutering ($90-200), vaccinations ($80-300), and the cost of various pet equipment and accessories such as food and water bowls, a dog bed, a leash and harness ($250-500).

Initial Costs of Keeping a Goldendoodle	
Purchase Price	$1,400-3,000 (around $250-300 for adoptions)
Spaying or Neutering	$90-200
Vaccinations	$80-300
Dog Accessories and Equipment	$250-500

All this is apart from the annual recurring costs of food, medical checkups, grooming, and even training costs. Below you will find a general estimate of some of the annual expenses that you can expect to cut into your budget. Please take note that these are only general ballpark figures, and

Chapter Two: Things to Know Before Getting a Goldendoodle

are adjustable depending on the price ranges in your area of products and services.

Annual Expenses for Keeping a Goldendoodle	
Dog Food	$150-500
Veterinary/Medical Costs	$160-670
Supplies	$150-1,700
Training	$30-500
Grooming Costs	$20-400
Miscellaneous Yearly Expenses (licenses, boarding, etc.)	$100-500

Of course, having a pet as lovable as a Goldendoodle is not just an investment of money, but also of love. For some people, having a pet in the house to help them de-stress, provide loyal and loving companionship, and even a kind of psychological security might actually translate to savings in terms of their own medical costs. Keeping a pet can help lower your stress levels, keep depression at bay, and can also keep a person healthier physically, mentally, and emotionally.

Chapter Two: Things to Know Before Getting a Goldendoodle

What are the Pros and Cons of Goldendoodles?

Still on the fence about getting a Goldendoodle? Perhaps the high purchase price is making you have second thoughts. One of the best ways to determine whether or not a Goldendoodle is the right dog for you is to have a brief overview of the pros and cons of keeping a dog, and a Goldendoodle in particular. This will allow you to keep the big picture in mind as you attempt to make up your mind on whether or not it is feasible for you to add a Goldendoodle to your home situation.

Pros for the Goldendoodle Breed

- A fairly predictable temperament in comparison with other mixed designer dog hybrids. This is an affectionate, friendly crossbreed, playful, and even goofy at times. They make great family pets.
- If you find the right dog that can be trained to serve as an aid dog, and with a hypo-allergenic coat to boot (take note that not all Goldendoodles may fit this profile!), it is a priceless combination of the best of two purebred dog qualities

Chapter Two: Things to Know Before Getting a Goldendoodle

- Goldendoodles live for a fairly long time, which means that that initial investment of a purchase price can be worth the companion of a lifetime
- This is an intelligent breed, fairly easy to train, and eager to please their human families. Both Poodles and Golden Retrievers have a long history of great camaraderie and loyal devotion to their human families.

Cons for the Goldendoodle Breed

- Goldendoodles can be fairly high maintenance in terms of grooming - aside from regular brushing, you will probably also have to pay a visit to a professional groomers every couple of months or so.
- Goldendoodles, as a breed, are unfortunately at risk of contracting a great number of health conditions or diseases - congenital traits from both Golden Retriever and Poodle breeds. The risk can be minimized through responsible breeding programs and a battery of health checks, but the possibility of a wide range of illnesses will still be there.
- Goldendoodles are not always hypo-allergenic, which means they are not always a feasible choice for people suffering with allergies. And because of the varying results of crossbreeding while this breed is still

Chapter Two: Things to Know Before Getting a Goldendoodle

relatively new, even puppies with hypo-allergenic coats may not always be temperamentally suited to being guide dogs. There is still an element of uncertainty and unpredictability in the kind of Goldendoodle you will be getting (as opposed to the predictability of purebreds)

- This is an expensive breed, which in itself might be off-putting to some.
- Goldendoodles are not recognized by any international dog organization or association. Being a relatively new crossbreed, there is much that is still unknown about Goldendoodles, which consequently decreases the factor of predictability in what you are getting with one of these dogs.

Chapter Three: Purchasing Your Goldendoodle

Now that you know a little bit more about the Goldendoodle breed, you are probably wondering where you can get one, how much it would cost, and how to pick a good and responsible breeder.

Where you get or purchase a Goldendoodle does require a bit of thought. Because of the recent popularity of, and demand for, designer dogs such as the Goldendoodle, there have been a great number of puppy mills that have proliferated, who make a business of breeding and selling

Chapter Three: Purchasing Your Goldendoodle

puppies, driven only by the potential profits. After all, nowadays, designer dogs can easily sell for twice the price of a purebred dog.

But how do you know you are getting a healthy puppy. This is certainly a legitimate question because irresponsible breeders will just keep producing puppies to sell, regardless of the health of the dam and sire, or the puppies. You certainly don't want to have a puppy that comes with a variety of health conditions, and you certainly don't want to support puppy mills and irresponsible breeders by providing them with easy business.

Bringing a Goldendoodle home is a big commitment - your dog will be a part of your family for the next 10-15 years, and he will share in your family's joys and triumphs for his entire lifetime. Putting in a little more thought, discretion and effort into finding a good breeder can prove worthwhile for you both for the next several years.

Where Can You Buy a Goldendoodle?

Before setting your sights on finding a Goldendodle breeder, you might want to consider adopting a rescue first. Not only will this cost less, but you will also have changed the life of a dog needing a good owner and a good home.

Chapter Three: Purchasing Your Goldendoodle

Typically, adopting a dog costs around $100-250, which is a far cry from the price that Goldendoodles usually command in the market. The following is a list of recues specializing in rehoming or placing abandoned or homeless Goldendoodles, and they can be a good starting point as you search for your future family member:

Dood Needing Homes. Goldendoodles.com. <http://goldendoodles.com/rehomedoods.htm>

IDOG Rescue. <http://idogrescue.com/>

Doodle Trust. <http://www.doodletrust.com/>

Doodle Rescue Collective Inc. <http://doodlerescue.org/>

Or you can simply visit your nearest dog shelter or rescue to see if they have any Goldendoodles. Even if you don't find the Goldendoodle you're looking for, you might find another dog breed you like that is in need of a home. Any time any dog finds an owner willing to take them in is always good.

How to Choose a Reputable Goldendoodle Breeder

If you would rather find a Goldendoodle puppy from a reputable breeder, then your next step is making a list of Goldendoodle breeders near your area. After you've made

Chapter Three: Purchasing Your Goldendoodle

out a prospective list, it is time to narrow down that list by contacting and visiting each one.

This is the time for you to exercise your discerning and good judgment. It will take a bit of extra effort to narrow down your choices, but it will prove worthwhile in the end. Although this can translate to a more expensive puppy, you will at least be assured of getting a Goldendoodle puppy that has been bred for healthy parents, was born and raised in a positive and healthy environment, has little or minimal risk of contracting hereditary or contagious diseases, and one that has had a good start in acquiring socialization skills.

While it is up to you to make your decision as to which breeder you feel you can trust - an important factor since you will likely have to reach out and communicate with him several times during your puppy's life, especially during in the beginning, there are a few guidelines you can adhere to as you make your decision:

- First of all, ask about the health and genetic screenings that the dam and sire have gone through. Satisfy your curiosity about the prospective parents as much as you want - including how often they are bred, when was their last litter, their age, and how many times they have given birth. Chances are, a reputable breeder will not mind, and might even enjoy, telling you about the selected dam and sire.

Chapter Three: Purchasing Your Goldendoodle

- Have a conversation about Goldendoodles. Goldendoodles are a relatively new breed whose characteristics have not yet been established, which means that there is still a lot of space for conjecture when it comes to Goldendoodle quirks and characteristics. You might not expect the breeder to know *everything* about Goldendoodles, but a genuine passion and dedication to the breed is not something that can be faked. A good breeder will be upfront and open with you regarding the pros and cons of the breed, possible health concerns, and what he may or may not still know.
- When possible, schedule a visit of the premises. You will want to see for yourself where the dogs are kept and in what condition. Take a look around. Is it clean? Do the dogs seem happy and content? This means that the breeder cares enough about her dogs to provide them with a clean living space that is insulated as much as possible from contamination and bacteria.
- Pay attention to how she deals with her dogs. Is she attentive, affectionate, and concerned about their welfare? The way she treats her dogs will probably be similar to how she will treat the mother and the puppies during the time after birth and before the puppies are being weaned. You will want well-adjusted and socialized puppies, so a hands-on

breeder with a constant presence around her dogs is a big plus.

If you have any other questions, don't hesitate to ask the breeder about it. On your end, you should also do your research, read information resources regarding the breed so that you can have an intelligent and two-way conversation with her, instead of the meeting being more about you grilling her as a breeder. Remember that you are not the only one being assessed here - a responsible breeder will also be interested in the prospective family with which she will be placing her puppies, so she will naturally prefer those who have taken the trouble to read up and learn more about the Goldendoodle breed.

Once you have made your decision, ask about the process of adopting or purchasing a puppy. You will likely be asked to make a deposit, and certain papers or contracts might be signed. Pay the required deposits, and settle down to wait for when the puppies will be ready.

Tips for Selecting a Healthy Goldendoodle Puppy

The good news is that if you've found a good breeder, then you can reasonably expect that all the puppies in her litter will be equally healthy and well-adjusted, regardless of which puppy you choose. The process of selecting your

Chapter Three: Purchasing Your Goldendoodle

puppy, therefore, really began when you first set about selecting a good and trusted Goldendoodle breeder.

But how do you go about selecting the Goldendoodle puppy that is the right one for you? This is mostly a personal choice, of course, and may depend largely on what you are looking for. Perhaps you will base your selection on the puppy's color, size, coat texture, or some other physical factor. If you isolated Goldendoodles as a breed because of their touted hypoallergenic coats, then you might ask for a hair sample to test out with whoever in your family has allergies before finalizing your choice and bringing the puppy home. Remember that not all Goldendoodles will have hypo-allergenic coats. Some do, but the only real way to find out which one does is to test their actual coats or hair.

If you don't have any preference, however, and want only a reasonably healthy puppy, then here are a few tips to guide you as you select your future canine family member:

- You want a puppy who is active, playful, attentive and curious. This allows you to isolate a puppy with fully functioning reflexes and the mental capacity to be curious about the things around him. A friendly temperament or disposition is also ideal.
- The well-socialized puppy will not hide from or shy away from you when you approach them. He will instead be curious about you, and will be quite docile if handled. This means that he has had sufficient

Chapter Three: Purchasing Your Goldendoodle

human contact to provide the good beginnings of proper socialization skills.

- Some owners choose the puppies who push forward to meet them, thinking that this means that it is the puppies who choose them. Be careful about this, however, because it can also mean that you are getting a puppy with a pushy temperament. While this can be quite adorable among puppies, remember that these puppies will eventually grow up, too. Do you really want to be sharing living space with a dog that might be temperamentally predisposed to being pushy or demanding of attention?
- Pay attention to how the puppy deals with the breeder, his mother, and his littermates. Again, this pertains more to the socialization skills that have already been conditioned into the puppy's temperamental makeup. Ideally, the puppy should be playful but not too aggressive, friendly, but also confident.
- Physically, examine the puppy carefully for possible signs of illness. The coat should be clean and soft, the body full and plump, and the eyes and nose clear of discharges. His eyes should actively follow movement - which you can test by holding out a finger a short distance away from his face and slowly moving it from side to side. Examine their feet, their

ears, and even beneath their tail to have a good idea of their state of cleanliness and physical condition.

Puppy-Proofing Your Home

Ideally, you should already have prepared your home a few days or weeks before your puppy is due to arrive. Puppy-proofing your home is not unlike child-proofing your home. Your basic concern is the safety of the little one, and making sure that they do not accidentally get into any trouble or suffer from any house accidents.

The difference, of course, is that a puppy will be far more mobile and will be more able to get into small nooks and corners than a toddler. Take a moment to look around your house and try to see it from the perspective of a puppy on an adventure of exploration. You can get onto all fours if this will help you. Look around. If you see something that can potentially be dangerous to your puppy, secure it or put into storage where it will not be easy for a puppy to get to.

Some of the things to watch out for include:

- Toxic or harmful plants
- Cleaning solutions
- Medicine

Chapter Three: Purchasing Your Goldendoodle

- Small objects such as balls, paper clips and the like which a puppy might get it into his head to swallow, and which can eventually lodge in his throat
- Dangling electrical cords, curtain cords, or floor-length curtains or table cloths. Dangling from or getting tied up in these fabrics or cords is just one potential pitfall. You don't want a puppy chewing into an electrical cord and getting electrocuted, and you certainly don't want the scenario of a puppy accidentally getting strangled by dangling cords. On the other hand, they might pull at a long tablecloth, taking all of the contents on the surface of the table down to the floor with it.
- Precious and breakable items and important papers or documents should be safely stored away.
- Open sources of water such as water tanks or even the toilet bowl should be safely sealed.
- Secure open fireplaces
- Put a small gate, rails, or fence around stairways, open balustrades, high terraces, and the like
- Secure food containers, and also the trash bin

There may be a host of other items around your home which can be potentially dangerous to, or in danger around, a roving and energetic puppy. Of course this will largely depend on what you have inside your home, but as a general rule, it is best to make your home clean, organized

Chapter Three: Purchasing Your Goldendoodle

and clutter-free in preparation for the arrival of your Goldendoodle puppy.

Chapter Three: Purchasing Your Goldendoodle

Chapter Four: Caring for Your New Goldendoodle

Before you settle into your home with your new Goldendoodle, you may want to take a look around your living space to determine whether or not it is conducive for a pet. Taking care of a pet isn't just about providing them with sufficient food and grooming them regularly. They should also be able to live well, and that means sufficient living space and opportunities for regular exercise.

Chapter Four: Caring for Your New Goldendoodle

In this chapter, we take a look at the ideal living conditions within which a Goldendoodle might thrive, and how much daily exercise this dog breed needs. Please keen in mind though that the suggestions in this chapter will necessarily be stated in general terms, because Goldendoodles still do vary greatly in size. There are large and standard sized Goldendoodles, and there are also smaller sized or miniature Goldendoodles. In terms of space and exercise requirements, smaller dogs generally require less compared to bigger sized dogs.

Ideal Habitat Requirements for Goldendoodles

It is always best for any family dogs to have free access to a fenced in yard wherein they can get regular exercise and explore outdoors within safe conditions. This is a breed that will thrive in an urban setting or farm. If you live in an apartment or a city, however, there are ways of making pet ownership workable.

Thankfully, the Goldendoodle is a gentle and temperamentally calm breed, and they are not generally high-energy dogs. Within your apartment or house, make sure that they have enough running space and a spot of their own where there is sufficient room for their bed, an assortment of toys, a crate if needed, and sufficient

Chapter Four: Caring for Your New Goldendoodle

opportunity to romp around or play if they wish. Despite being a calm dog in general, they will certainly enjoy daily activities such as running, walking, or any suitable game or play to keep fit mentally and physically, and to be able to channel their energies productively. If they do not have enough opportunity or space to play or run around, their energy can turn destructive.

If your Goldendoodle does not have ready access to a safely-enclosed and open area, make sure that he gets a few hours of moderate exercise such as walking every day. Get him used to the feel of a leash and harness early on so that he will be amenable to wearing them during your regular walks. If weather conditions permit outdoor walking, then make sure he at least gets some hours of indoor playing such with various interactive toys.

Supplies and Equipment to Have on Hand

Invest in quality dog equipment and accessories early on. Not only will these last for a good many years, good quality beds, food and water bowls, and grooming equipment will also help to promote an overall healthy dog. Besides which, it can make your Goldendoodle feel welcome and not so timid and shy if he has his own personal spot and things which can serve as his safe spot.

Chapter Four: Caring for Your New Goldendoodle

Among the various tools or equipment that you should readily have at home include:

- Crate or carrier
- Blanket or dog bed
- Food and water dishes
- Toys (assortment)
- Collar, leash and harness
- Grooming supplies
- Dog food and treats

The uses of each are pretty self-explanatory. A blanket with a firm support can give him a good and restful place to sleep, and clean and quality food and water bowls or dishes that are easy to clean and sanitize will also promote healthy eating. Quality grooming supplies -which you will be using regularly, may also promote good coat and skin health and texture, and a suitable leash and harness will adjust to your dog's size as he grows, and be a convenient way to attach your dog's identification tags whenever you venture out of doors.

Provide him with an assortment of toys to begin with. You'll likely find him gravitating to one or another of those toys, and these will be his favorite. Oftentimes, though, it is a good idea to have a variety of them ready at hand to shake things up a little in your regular bonding moments.

Chapter Four: Caring for Your New Goldendoodle

Exercise Requirements for the Goldendoodle

Goldendoodles require daily but moderate and non-strenuous exercises such as daily walking. It has also been found that many Goldendoodles gravitate towards the water - likely an inherited propensity from their Golden Retriever ancestor - so swimming is a definite exercise possibility for your pooch. Swimming is also a good alternative daily exercise to walking, especially if you want to give his joints and legs a little rest from too much walking.

Goldendoodles are also quite intelligent, easy to train and eager to learn, so some mental stimulation through obedience training is also in order.

Goldendoodles are also quite sociable, and they will enjoy spending their time with you. Being exposed to dog parks where there are other people with dogs can also help him in continuously developing his social skills. This is where their training can come in handy, though - because Goldendoodles do have a certain stubborn streak, which can be coupled with a propensity for barking and guarded aggression towards strangers. Habitual obedience training can keep them disciplined and well-behaved even when the two of you are in a public place.

Chapter Four: Caring for Your New Goldendoodle

In general, however, this is a friendly breed that is more likely to be friendly with strangers, which means that they won't really make good or reliable guard dogs.

Chapter Five: Meeting Your Goldendoodle's Nutritional Needs

A nutritious and balanced diet is the cornerstone to your dog's good health. But how do you know that your dog is getting all the nutrients that he needs?

Most high-quality commercial dog food will be able to provide all that your dog needs, since these were formulated with this principle in mind. But sometimes, we do not always understand what makes a good and healthy diet for dogs. Some 30 years ago, it was believed that dogs were carnivores and that an "all meat" diet was best for

Chapter Five: Meeting Your Goldendoodle's Nutritional Needs

them. We know better now (dogs are omnivores and require more nutrients that cannot be supplied by an all-meat diet), and so pet food formulations have evolved accordingly. But we are learning new things everyday, and our understanding of canine nutrition and health still continues to evolve.

This chapter sets out basic information and principles regarding the nutritional needs of dog, but as a pet owner, it is important that you also continue to educate yourself regarding any news or developments in this field. Read, read, read! Ask questions, be discerning, consult with your veterinarian, network with other dog owners, but most important of all, pay attention to your dog's state of health. Many times, the various health conditions that may affect our dogs can be traced back to the food he eats. In a very real way, this is not so different from humans, either. Sometimes our dog's state of health can be our best gauge in determining whether or not they are getting all the nutritional needs they require.

The Nutritional Needs of Dogs

There are six essential nutrients which a dog needs, and which they can get from their food. These six classes of

Chapter Five: Meeting Your Goldendoodle's Nutritional Needs

nutrients are the building blocks of canine nutrition, and they serve to provide your Goldendoodle with sufficient energy, cell growth and regeneration, and supported bodily functions, among others.

These six essential nutrients include:

Water

Like humans, majority of a dog's body composition - about 70%, in fact - is composed of water. Dehydration is thus a very real danger if you do not provide him plenty of readily available drinking water on a daily basis.

Proteins

Mainly obtained from meat and most meat-based products, protein is essential for growth and cell regeneration and repair, and for Goldendoodles, are necessary in the maintenance of their beautiful coat or fur. In general, adult dogs require at least 18-25 percent of protein in their diet.

Carbohydrates

This is usually derived from fiber-based products, and help in maintaining the intestinal health of your pet. Some carbohydrates can even be a good source of energy for your pet. Examples of these are wheat, barley, corn, and oats.

Chapter Five: Meeting Your Goldendoodle's Nutritional Needs

Fats

Fats provide your pet with a concentrated source of energy, and are also essential for some vitamins (A, E, D and K) to be absorbed. They help in protecting the internal organs and are vital in cellular production. Fats generally account for about 10-15 % of an adult dog's diet. Anything in excess, such as calories from table scraps and treats) may lead to weight problems and obesity.

Vitamins and Minerals

Vitamins and minerals usually cannot be synthesized by a dog's body, so the primary source of these are the synthesized versions obtainable in commercially available quality dog foods. Vitamins and minerals help in the normal functioning of their bodies, and also helps maintain their bones and teeth.

Daily Energy Requirements

As you continue to read more literature and information regarding canine nutrition, you may come across the acronym RER. This stands for Resting Energy Requirement, and is the closest that experts have devised in a determination on how much dog food to feed each individual dog.

Chapter Five: Meeting Your Goldendoodle's Nutritional Needs

The truth is that there is no standard formula for how much to feed your dog that is true for all dogs in every circumstance. A simple look at different packages of pet food will attest to this - their advise can range from 1 cup to over two cup each day. And then of course, you have to consider the dog's daily energy consumption, their stage in life and the unique nutritional needs they may have at their time of life such as adulthood, pregnancy, adolescence, and entering their senior years.

Resting Energy Requirement, or RER, is a determination of your dog's energy consumption while he is at rest, and this is determined by a formula that takes into consideration his body weight. For dogs that weigh between 2 and 45 kg (5-99 lbs), the formula is as follows:

RER = 30 (body weight in kilograms) + 70

This is your dog's daily calorie needs on any given day. But the problem is confounded when, for all practical purposes, he stops being "at rest." When he undertakes various other activities such as light to heavy exercise, or if he is simply going through life changes such as pregnancy or lactation, weaning, neutering, or weight loss, then his energy needs would necessarily increase. Take note that the variable factors in this case are not simply internal but also external - changes in the weather and temperature, for

Chapter Five: Meeting Your Goldendoodle's Nutritional Needs

instance, illnesses and health conditions, or changed living conditions, also serve to modify his basic RER.

Below is a table illustrating some of these variables and how these affect your dog's prescribed daily caloric intake and RER:

Neutered Adult	RER x 1
Intact Adult	RER x 1.6
Moderate Work Adult	RER x 3
Pregnant dog in the last 21 days before birth	RER x 3
Weaning Puppy	RER x 3
Adolescent Puppy	RER x 2
Obese Puppy undergoing weight loss activities	RER x 1

Confused? This is understandable, all the more so because the implications are that you will need to make regular dietary changes to your dog's caloric intake depending on variables that change constantly. Even the experts will not profess to state that there is a standard and reliable formula by which you can measure what is recommended daily food intake for dogs.

Chapter Five: Meeting Your Goldendoodle's Nutritional Needs

But perhaps it does not need to be so confusing. In much the same way that we make adjustments to what and how much we eat on any given day based on various physical, emotional and psychological factors we go through, so do we also need to make similar adjustments to your dog's diet. Some days they may have worked hard and deserve to eat more, or some days you may consider limiting their portion if all they've been doing is lying on the couch. Perhaps it isn't a mathematical or scientific matter, but a sympathetic one.

Simply pay attention. If you find that your dog seems thin and listless, try and increase his daily food intake a little. If you notice him growing a bit bulky around the middle, reduce his portion. Please remember, though, that you should not make any drastic changes to your dog's diet without first consulting with your veterinarian.

How to Select a Quality Dog Food Brand

It isn't easy to pick out the best dog food for your Goldendoodle, and even if you think you may have picked the right one, there is always new information and new dog food products being launched that claim to be the best that can make you second-think your initial choice. After all,

Chapter Five: Meeting Your Goldendoodle's Nutritional Needs

why stick to what is tried and tested if there are other choices that could be healthier? The question is, of course, whether or not it actually is healthier. How can you tell?

While this book does not promote or endorse a single dog food brand, we can present you with some basic guidelines in choosing the right dog food for your Goldendoodle. The only other thing you need to do is to be able to read dog food labels because, once you know what you're looking for, the package itself should tell you all you need to know.

That said, it is always a good idea to stay up-to-date with news and breakthroughs in the field of dog nutrition, and you can also network with other dog owners, especially those who own Goldendoodles as pets - and compare notes. You might also want to ask your trusty vet what dog food brand he recommends. This is a good way to share your interests with other like-minded people, while at the same staying informed in the field of canine nutrition.

- To start with, all dog foods must meet FDA safety regulations, and come with an AAFCO nutritional adequacy statement. This means that the dog food is safe for canine consumption, and that it meets the minimum nutritional requirements of your dog.

Chapter Five: Meeting Your Goldendoodle's Nutritional Needs

- Pick a dog food brand that has been especially formulated for your dog type, whether a puppy, a senior, an adult, or a pregnant and lactating mother.
- Dogs are omnivores, which means that while they can survive on a diet of meat and vegetables, experts are mostly in agreement that is is healthier for dogs to be on a meat-based diet to supply them with high quality protein. As a rule, dogs don't really need carbohydrates - and potatoes, starches or other grains are usually put in to offset the meat content. Whole grains like brown rice are a good choice, however, if you cannot find one that is grain-free.
- Avoid pet foods that contain corn or soy, as these do not really have any nutritive content. Steer clear of artificial colors flavors, sweeteners and preservatives.
- When looking at the ingredients list, remember that pet food manufacturers are legally obligated to list the ingredients in descending order based on weight. That means that the first item on their ingredients list is the primary component of the dog food. Ideally, it should be meat that is identified by the meat source such as chicken, lamb or turkey. This ensures that you are getting quality meat, and not meat meals or meat that comes from unidentified sources.

Chapter Five: Meeting Your Goldendoodle's Nutritional Needs

A good and balanced nutritious diet is the cornerstone to a happy and healthy Goldendoodle. As with most dietary choices that involve your pet, however, your best basis is your Goldendoodle's state of health, and how his daily diet affects his daily energy levels and physical condition. Is he lethargic? Is he listless? Is his coat clean and luxuriously healthy? Does he have sufficient energy for his day to day exercise and play? Does he suffer from a lack of appetite? Be cautious in making any sort of dietary changes, but at the same time, be attentive and observant of your Goldendoodle's state of health and wellbeing.

Dangerous Foods to Avoid

It can be tempting to feed your dog treats and table scraps, but this is not always advisable. There are certain human foods that are, in fact, dangerous for our four legged friends. We may not always be aware of this because owners might think that if we can eat it, then so can our dogs. Be warned, however, that certain substances can be downright dangerous for dogs.

Should your Goldendoodle ingest any of the following foods, please call emergency services immediately.

- Alcohol
- Apple seeds

Chapter Five: Meeting Your Goldendoodle's Nutritional Needs

- Avocado
- Cherry pits
- Chocolate
- Citrus
- Coconut
- Coffee
- Garlic
- Grapes/raisins
- Hops
- Macadamia nuts
- Milk and Dairy
- Mold
- Mushrooms
- Mustard seeds
- Onions/leeks
- Peach pits
- Potato leaves/stems
- Raw meat and eggs
- Rhubarb leaves
- Salty snacks
- Tea
- Tomato leaves/stems
- Walnuts
- Xylitol
- Yeast dough

Chapter Five: Meeting Your Goldendoodle's Nutritional Needs

Chapter Six: Training Your Goldendoodle

An important part of your relationship with your Goldendoodle is training. Dog training is no longer viewed as a privilege for those dog owners who can afford it - people are increasingly beginning to learn the importance of training for a healthy and happy dog.

While Goldendoodles have initially been bred specifically to act as a guide dog, not all Doodles will find

Chapter Six: Training Your Goldendoodle

themselves taking on this position in their human community. Does this mean that training is no longer necessary for them? Not really. Most experts have found that training your dog not only helps build the bond between you and your pet, it also provides your animal best friend with necessary mental stimulation, it prevents or at least minimizes problem behaviors, it teaches them proper socialization, and it may even save your dog's life. Take, for instance, a scenario where your dog slips from his collar while you are out walking him. Instead of running wildly through the streets and perhaps rushing onto incoming traffic, a firm command from you to heel, sit and stay can prevent potential tragedy.

The level of your dog's training may increase depending on your patience and capacity to teach. Goldendoodles are naturally intelligent, and you might be surprised how quickly he is able to learn various commands and many other tricks you can teach him. Or, in the alternative, you can also enroll him in an obedience school to be taught by professionals. Just make sure that he undergoes positive reinforcement training, as Goldendoodles are known to react negatively to dominance or punishment-based teaching methods.

The process of training should begin as early as possible, as you teach your puppy some essential skills that would make your relationship with him hassle and stress-free. In this chapter, you will find information regarding

Chapter Six: Training Your Goldendoodle

basic training lessons such as socialization, housebreaking and crate training. We also take a look at what positive reinforcement techniques mean, and what they consist of.

Socializing Your New Goldendoodle Puppy

It is critical that the process of socialization should start early. There is a brief window of opportunity for socializing a puppy - and this window ends at around 16-20 weeks of age. After this time, it is difficult, if not impossible, to teach a dog or a puppy crucial socialization skills. We call them crucial because the alternative is a stressful life for the puppy, who is fearful of and distrustful of strange and unfamiliar objects, people, sights, and sounds. For dogs coexisting with humans in the human world, where each day is filled with what would appear to be strange and unfamiliar sights and sounds, life would be very stressful indeed for our four-legged friend. This stress may manifest itself in constant fear, anxiety, or even aggression - all of which could have been avoided if the proper time and effort was devoted to socializing them in their early weeks.

The socialization process itself is not very complicated, and may even prove enjoyable. Starting at around three weeks of age, the young puppies should be handled daily by the breeder, and by as many different people as possible. These periods of human contact can start

Chapter Six: Training Your Goldendoodle

out in brief periods of time, gradually increasing, until the puppy begins to learn that there is nothing to fear from human contact. Handling them in as many different ways as possible - gently, of course - should also set the stage for proper grooming processes later in the puppy's life.

Aside from human contact, socialization also involves a gradual introduction to strange places, sights, sounds, and even other animals. Newborn puppies are naturally confined to a single room in the beginning, but as they grow and begin to be curious about the bigger world, you can gradually begin to introduce them to other parts of the house, carefully supervised, and all done within a positive atmosphere. If you are bringing a puppy home for the first time, you might begin by confining them to a single room to begin with. Allow them some time to become familiar with your presence and the room he is in. Later on, as his confidence develops, you can gradually begin introducing him to the other rooms of the house. Eventually, you may bring him out to the yard, and later on, after he has become familiar to the feel of a leash, a walk outdoors. The wider the range of experiences you expose him to, the better his chances of developing into a well-adjusted dog.

The basic principle is fairly simple: it involves gradual but steady exposure to as many sights, sounds and smells as possible, all done within a positive environment. This teaches them that there is nothing to fear about humans or strange and unfamiliar objects and places. Allow them to

Chapter Six: Training Your Goldendoodle

explore and to satisfy their curiosity, all the while providing your presence as a reassurance of safety and security.

If you have other pets such as another dog or a cat, create supervised introductory encounters between your new puppy and the rest of your household. Always make sure that these are pleasant and positive encounters, as this reinforces the puppy's perception that he is welcome in your home, and that there are no immediate threats in his environment of which he need be afraid.

This does not mean, however, that you should always be a constant presence in your puppy's life. You might also leave him alone for short periods of time, gradually increasing this time little by little every day. This would teach your puppy that there is nothing to fear about being left alone, and enables him to avoid separation anxiety later on in life.

Housebreaking your Goldendoodle Puppy

One of the undoubted cornerstones of a good and healthy relationship with your Goldendoodle is housebreaking. There are some owners for whom an inability to abide by housebreaking rules can make or break a relationship with their dog. But this need not be so. With proper training, your Goldendoodle can easily be housebroken, and this is true whether you have a puppy or

Chapter Six: Training Your Goldendoodle

an adult dog. All you need to remember is to practice patience and consistency

There are three popular methods for housebreaking training:

- regular trips outdoors
- paper training
- crate training

To reinforce housebreaking training, it is advisable to keep your dog on a regular meal schedule - this allows their digestion to work at a regular and expected pace, and this also supports a regular schedule for your dog to go. Regardless of which training method you choose, keep them to a predictable and consistent feeding schedule so that their times of going to the bathroom will also be at predictable and consistent times.

If you have a fenced in backyard, then allowing your dog outside of the house at regular intervals allows them to go when they are outside of the house. Pay attention to how soon they urinate or defecate soon after feeding, and simply make this a habitual time for them to be outdoors. Should they meet your expectations and take their bathroom break while they are outdoors, reinforce this habit with rewards such as praise or treats.

Paper training, on the other, or the use of puppy pads, may not be an ideal training method for many, but may prove necessary in certain living situations - such as when the dog cannot be let outside due to bad weather conditions, or when you simply cannot be home to let them

Chapter Six: Training Your Goldendoodle

out. This is also a good starting point in housebreaking puppies whom you cannot let out out of the house because they are still too young. The principle is to teach them to go only in a specific spot (the paper or puppy pad), and not anywhere else in the house. This would be an "approved" spot for them to go. With proper training, the puppy will soon begin to associate the paper or pad with their designated bathroom, and they will not do their business elsewhere. As they grow a little bit older, you can then modify your technique and retrain them by going outdoors or through the crate training method.

    The third training method, or crate training, is by far the most popular method to date among dog owners. Crate training involves confining your dog to a reasonably sized crate which is large enough for them to move around in, but not too large that they begin to designate a corner as their bathroom. The principle is that dogs are clean creatures who will not want to go in the same place where they sleep and lie down. They will usually let you know by behavioral signs such as whining and scratching that she wishes to go outside the crate. You should be ready to act immediately because the interval might not be too long before he does go. Take him outside immediately, and if he does, reward him. He then learns that it is not okay to go in the same place where he sleeps, and that he should catch your attention if he wishes to go outside. Over time, this should grow into a habit with reasonable expectations: that you expect him to do his business outside of the house, and that he should catch your attention so that you can let him out when he needs to.

Chapter Six: Training Your Goldendoodle

Positive Reinforcement for Obedience Training

Whether you are housebreaking your puppy, getting him used to a leash and collar, or training him to obey basic commands, experts recommend the use of positive reinforcement rather than dominance or punishment methods.

Not only will this reinforce the bond between you and your Goldendoodle, this creates a positive learning experience for your dog so that he is eager to learn more, and eager to please you by learning as quickly as possible. This is a good way to work with training Goldendoodles because of their natural eagerness to please, and their natural sensitivity which makes them averse to, and react negatively, to punishment-based training methods.

Positive training methods work on the basis of certain principles, including the following:

- The performance of desired behavior should be rewarded immediately to help them associate the desired behavior with pleasant connotations. Timing is everything, they say. The trick is to reward them immediately after the desired behavior so that the link and association between the behavior and the reward is built and reinforced.

Chapter Six: Training Your Goldendoodle

- While traditionally rewards have been given in the form of treats, the increasing incidence of obesity among various dog breeds have made treats a not-so-viable option for rewards training. While you can still use treats as rewards - especially in the beginning - supplement, and later on replace, this with other forms of rewards such as praise or affection. As long as they associate the desired behavior with something positive, the principle of rewards training still works.

- Be consistent, make training regular until it becomes a habit, but make your training sessions short and fun. Don't make things more complicated than they need to be for your dog. Keep it short and simple - and this includes the commands you give them. Brief and fun training sessions that ideally end in a positive note - done regularly and consistently - can be a more effective training method than trying to hammer certain commands into your dog for hours at a time.

- Remember that training sessions are also bonding sessions between you and your pet, and it is also a period within which you communicate and try to understand each other. This is therefore a two-way street. You should also pay attention to your dog's mood and behavior. If your dog becomes bored and uninterested during training, trying to prolong the training session unnecessarily will defeat your

Chapter Six: Training Your Goldendoodle

purpose as he will begin to view these times with negative associations.

- The most important thing is to have fun. Training your dog isn't just for his benefit, it is also for yours. Enjoy your dog's company during this time. If you view training your dog from the proper perspective, you'll probably be pleasantly surprised at just how smart and intelligent your dog is.

Chapter Seven: Grooming Your Goldendoodle

Goldendoodles come in a variety of coat types, of which there are three: wavy, fleece, and curly. Being a relatively new breed, the coat types of Goldendoodles are still not what would be called "standard," and the variations in their coats largely depends upon which are more dominant, the genes of their Golden Retriever, or Poodle, parent.

These three coat types that prevail among Goldendoodles have distinct characteristics:

Chapter Seven: Grooming Your Goldendoodle

- Wavy coats are hair-like in texture, and generally low-maintenance; shedding varies from dog to dog
- Fleece coats (borderline) are loose curls that are hair-like in texture, but soft to the touch; these require generally little care except when the adult hair is growing, during which time the coat requires a good deal of maintenance
- Curly coats (woolly coats) are tight curls that resemble that of a Poodle's, and require at least half an hour of daily grooming. Curly coats usually don't shed, however, and are generally allergy-friendly

Like with most designer dogs, a Goldendoodle's coat is unique and characteristic to this breed, and they do require regular grooming. It can approximate either a Golden Retriever's or a Poodle's coat (or somewhere in between), and both types do need to be maintained to keep the dog from developing matts or tangles.

It is recommended that you bring your Goldendoodle to a professional groomer's every few months for a trim. Some of the necessary trim is around the eyes, the beard, and the removal of excess hair from the ears, all of which help to maintain your dog's good health.

At home, periodic grooming is necessary. This chapter contains some of the basic guidelines in grooming Goldendoodles.

Chapter Seven: Grooming Your Goldendoodle

Recommended Tools to Have on Hand

You might want to invest in some quality grooming tools early on if you are raising and caring for Goldendoodles. This is also an excellent bonding time between you and your pet, especially if done within a positive environment. Starting a regular grooming habit when the Goldendoodle is still a puppy will not only build your relationship over time, it will also allow them to get used to, perhaps even enjoy, the bathing and grooming rituals. A clean and presentable Goldendoodle is also a healthy dog.

Below are some of the tools and equipment you will need in grooming your Goldendoodle:

- Slicker brush
- Thinning shears
- Clipper blades
- Nail Clippers
- Pin Brush
- Dog shampoo
- Dog nail clippers
- Dog toothpaste and toothbrush

While many of the basic grooming requirements will be performed for you by a professional groomer, it is always a good idea to learn how to care for and groom your Goldendoodle yourself, in the comfort of your own home.

Chapter Seven: Grooming Your Goldendoodle

You may not always have the luxury of always going to a groomer's, and while a visit to a professional every few months or so may be necessary, a Goldendoodle's coat requires more frequent care than that - some daily brushing if at all possible. Doing so can help prevent coat problems long-term, such as mats or tangles, which can promote the growth of bacteria or parasites, and the removal of which may be painful for your dog.

Tips for Bathing Goldendoodles

Once a month is a good regular schedule for bathing and shampooing your Goldendoodle. This can be done in a regular bathtub, or a raised tub. You might also want to provide nonslip bath mats on the floor and at the bottom of the tub. Use a high quality dog shampoo, or if preferred, a mild baby shampoo.

Make sure to avoid getting shampoo in your dog's eyes. You could use a soap-free washcloth to wash the face. And then starting from the head and work your way down and back, massage the shampoo into his coat. Lather along the back, neck, chest, belly and legs, all the way down to the tail. You may even want to use a comb at this time and work through the coat while he's lathered.

Chapter Seven: Grooming Your Goldendoodle

Rinse thoroughly, making sure that no shampoo residue is left in his coat. You may probably find a shower hose helpful as you rinse. Towel dry, and then use a blow dryer at low setting, using a slicker brush as you dry.

Tips for Grooming Your Goldendoodle

A Goldendoodle's hair can grow to as long as 4 to 8 inches if untrimmed. Brushing and combing regularly will keep their coat clean and neat, and will also stimulate the production of natural oils that help maintain their coat.

Using slicker brush, start at the bottom by separating a line of hair and brushing down from this line, gradually working your way up. Brushing the Goldendoodle's coat in this way will ensure that you eliminate all the mats and tangles.

Periodically, you will want to trim your Goldendoodle's hair, particularly around the eyes, the beard, to remove the excess hair from the ears, and between the foot pads. You might also want to snip off mats that may be beginning to form behind the ears and behind the elbows. Finish off by trimming from the belly and under the tail. If you are uncertain of how short to trim, you can bring your dog to a professional groomer and have them show you how to begin with.

Chapter Seven: Grooming Your Goldendoodle

There are some who also prefer to give their Goldendoodles periodic cuts or trims, following some of the more popular "cuts." This involves overall trimming and shaving, which really should be handled by a professional. Just remember that a Goldendoodle should never be completely shaved as their coats are necessary for protection and insulation.

Other Grooming Tasks

Aside from brushing and bathing your Goldendoodle, there are a few other grooming tasks that should be carried out regularly. These include dental care, trimming your Golden's nails, and cleaning his ears.

Brushing Your Goldendoodle's Teeth

It is best to start out the habit of brushing your dog's teeth when they are young. This allows them to form the habit of dental care early, as most adult dogs find the experience of a foreign object rubbing against their teeth strange and uncomfortable. But brushing your dog's teeth is necessary because it helps keep them away from tooth and gum disease, and the formation of cavities.

Chapter Seven: Grooming Your Goldendoodle

Use toothbrush specifically designed for dogs, and toothpaste that has been formulated for our canine friends. Remember that dogs cannot spit, so it is very likely that they will ingest some of the toothpaste as you work. Using cleaning agents formulated for humans can be harmful to your dog's health.

Brushing your dog's teeth is pretty straightforward. When you are just starting out, you can probably begin by using toothpaste applied on your finger or cotton swabs just to get them used to the idea of it. Place a small amount of the toothpaste on their outer lips so that they become accustomed to the smell and taste of it.

Be patient. This is a habit that you build over time. Lift the flaps of your dog's mouth to get at the teeth - in the beginning, you probably won't be able to reach past the front teeth, but this is okay. As your Goldendoodle begins to figure out that there is nothing threatening or scary about the process, he will allow you to reach deeper inside his mouth. Eventually, you may even reach as far as his back teeth.

Keep the entire process positive, using slow and gentle motions to clean his teeth. If he struggles and wants to get away, just let him. You can try again the next day. Eventually, he'll sit still long enough for you to finish. Whether or not he actually grows to enjoy the process, he will at least learn to tolerate it. If he has behaved impeccably, be sure to reward him with praises or a positive activity to further reinforce the habit.

Trimming Your Goldendoodle's Nails

As with brushing your dog's teeth, it is best to start trimming your dog's nails when they are young so that the habit is built early. If this is your first time to do so and are hesitant or afraid, have a professional groomer or a vet show you how it's done. It's a pretty direct and quick process, and with time, it will prove an easy grooming task to maintain, and should be done every two weeks or so.

It is best to be conservative in trimming your dog's nails, as you will not want to cut or injure the quick or the vessel that supplies blood to the nails. Be gentle in handling their feet and toes. Use nail clippers that are specific for dogs, don't use human nail clippers as these will not work, and might end up injuring your dog instead. Make sure that the clippers are sharp, and trim around, never across.

This is another important part of regular dog grooming because long toenails can be detrimental to your dog's physical condition. Toe nails that are too long can be twisted or be pushed back right into the nail bed, which can be quite painful for your Goldendoodle. When you start to hear your dog's nails clicking on the floor, that usually means that it is time for a trim.

Chapter Seven: Grooming Your Goldendoodle

Cleaning Your Goldendoodle's Ears

Goldendoodles typically have long and hanging ears that are covered with hair. And because of their size and shape, air flow is limited, and moisture can get trapped inside the ears, making it a fertile place for the growth of bacteria. The abundance of hair in the ears can also trap the moisture, which can increase the risk of infection. When you find a buildup of wax and dirt inside the ears, or if you notice a bad odor coming from your Goldendoodle's ears, it could be a sign of ear mites. Prevent these scenarios from happening in the first place by making a regular habit of cleaning your dog's ears.

As with most grooming techniques that require you to handle a dog's sensitive body parts, it behooves you to be gentle and cautious. The insides of a dog's ears are very sensitive, which means you should not handle this type of cleaning roughly or crudely. Avoid using q-tips, for instance, as the ends may poke the insides of his ears and injure him. Instead, use a cotton pad or ball soaked or moistened with an ear cleaning solution recommended by your vet. Wipe the insides of the ears gently and carefully, clean the folds, and make sure that it is clean and dry when you are finished.

Chapter Seven: Grooming Your Goldendoodle

There are those who also recommend plucking excess hair from inside the ears, but this is something that should be done by a professional groomer. It is certainly not a good field for experimentation, as most groomers have specialized equipment to deal with this.

Chapter Eight: Breeding Your Goldendoodle

To be blunt about it, a Goldendoodle, like most of the designer dogs that are currently so popular, are mutts. This is the more common term for hybrid dogs which are the offspring of two different breeds. The term "designer dog" is more of a label applied to dog hybrids resulting from the mix of two purebreds.

It can be said that most dog purebreds today were also once mutts. Some may have resulted naturally, while others were the result of intentional crossbreeding years ago by people who wanted dogs with desirable character traits that they sought to isolate through selective breeding. Several years later, once the breed has become "established,"

Chapter Eight: Breeding Your Goldendoodle

it becomes a recognized dog breed and a purebred. In dealing with purebred dogs, you know what you're getting in terms of size, weight, coat texture and coat colors, and even in temperament. By contrast, crossbreeding or attempting to create hybrid dogs can result in a great variety of characteristics among the puppies, depending upon which character traits of the parents are more dominant.

Breeding Goldendoodles and Designer Dogs

Goldendoodles are just one of many designer dogs that have grown in popularity in recent years - bolstered, no doubt, by their cute names and celebrity endorsements. One typically recognizes designer dogs by their unique names - a mash up of the names of the two purebred dogs that have produced the desired offspring. Goldendoodles, for instance, is a combination of Golden Retriever and Poodle. Many designer dogs involve crossbreeding with poodles because of the desirable hypoallergenic quality of a Poodle's coat.

First generation hybrid Goldendoodles have two purebred parents: one Golden Retriever and one a Poodle. First generation hybrids are often referred to as F1. Depending on the quality or characteristic which the breeder seeks to isolate, F1 generation Goldendoodles can be crossed with another Poodle, another Golden Retriever, or another Goldendoodle. Sometimes breeders may seek to introduce an "outcross" - or another breed entirely, usually to isolate

Chapter Eight: Breeding Your Goldendoodle

desired characteristics such as coat texture and quality, the dog's size, or the dog's temperament.

Goldendoodles are still a relatively new breed, and it may take years more before they are granted recognition by international dog organizations. The only way this can be done is through concerted efforts by responsible breeders in the establishment of a breed standard for Goldendoodles. At this point, however, there is no such thing. There is simply too many variations in the qualities and characteristics of Goldendoodles for there to be an established "standard" Goldendoodle. In many ways, nature will also be playing a role as this new hybrid crossbreed measures up against inherited traits, both positive and negative - including illnesses and health conditions from two or more different breeds.

This is why responsible breeding is so important. Responsible breeders will seek to isolate healthy dogs to breed - and while there are no absolute guarantees when it comes to health, risks can be minimized by making sure that the dogs you are breeding have no genetic conditions or illnesses that they can pass on to their offspring. Unfortunately, due to the high demand, the wide popularity, and the high cost of designer dogs, dog breeding has become a ripe field for unscrupulous breeders with puppy farms: breeding indiscriminately, regardless of the health and welfare of the dogs, and driven only by expected profits. You can help make sure that this practice does not

Chapter Eight: Breeding Your Goldendoodle

proliferate by purchasing from or supporting only reputable breeders who take the trouble to get health checks for the dogs they breed.

For that matter, if you do own a Goldendoodle and you are not intending to breed them, then please do the responsible thing and have them spayed or neutered. The number of unwanted and rescued dogs is growing each year, and this includes, unfortunately, many designer dogs such as Goldendoodles who have not been able to find good homes. If you do intend for them to have puppies, however, have your dog checked beforehand to determine if they are fit and healthy and do not suffer from any health conditions. And of course, it is always good to know more about the breeding process itself, of which you can find more about in the rest of this chapter.

Please also remember that responsible breeding works upon some general principles, the most basic of which is that one should always breed to improve the breed. Of course, this may not be such an easy thing to do for the Goldendoodle breed - for which there is no official breed standard. The next best thing you can do, therefore, is to network with Goldendoodle associations and breeders and learn more about what are the desirable traits associated with this breed are, and how best to isolate those desired characteristics. For the Goldendoodle, the initial intent for this crossbreed was to develop a guide dog that had the typical temperament and personality characteristics of the

Chapter Eight: Breeding Your Goldendoodle

Golden Retriever, while at the same time having a hypoallergenic coat similar to that of a Poodle.

It may be that you will not succeed in the first few generations - some have found that F1B Goldendoodles - or F1 Goldendoodles backcrossed to Poodles - were the generation as near as possible to this ideal. You may not be intending to be a professional Goldendoodle breeder, but networking is always a good place to start in helping to improve the breed overall. Breeders are always on the lookout for healthy Goldendoodles that are as close as possible from the ideal standard.

It is also imperative that breeding dogs - which includes the process of caring for the pregnant dam, caring for, weaning and raising the puppies, requires commitment and dedication. It will be costly, particularly when you consider the various genetic screening and health checks you will have to consider before the breeding process even begins. Should any complications arise, medical expenses can also pile up, not to mention the responsibility and consequent difficulty of finding homes for puppies that may or may not have health conditions.

If all this sounds unreasonably cautious for a process that is as natural as breeding, the increasing numbers of unwanted and homeless puppies (designer dogs included), should be enough to put you on the alert. That said, done correctly and responsibly, the raising of a litter of healthy

Chapter Eight: Breeding Your Goldendoodle

and beautiful Goldendoodles can be one of the most rewarding things in the world.

Basic Dog Breeding Information

The first step is of course choosing a suitable mating pair - both the dam and the sire should undergo all the appropriate health checks to be considered suitable. Make sure that their vaccinations are also current and up to date. And be observant also of the dog's temperament, since you are also looking for friendly, intelligent, loving, and loyal dogs that will hopefully breed true from their parents.

Tiny or miniature female dogs usually reach their age of first heat at around 6 months of age, while larger breed dogs can have their first heat at a later date, sometimes from 18 months to up to two years. Females will have recurring seasons of heat at intervals of approximately six months, or twice a year. Regardless, though, it is not recommended to breed females during their period of first heat. Motherhood takes a toll on the dog's physical and psychological reserves. She needs to be mature enough to handle the stresses of pregnancy and motherhood, and her body also needs to be fully developed to be able to handle pregnancy and lactation.

Males, on the other hand, typically become fertile as early as six months, but they reach sexual maturity at a later date - at around 12 to 15 months. From sexual maturity

Chapter Eight: Breeding Your Goldendoodle

onwards, they may be ready to mate at any time, but it does not always mean that they should. Like with females, males also do need to reach a certain maturity before being bred.

You will know when the female is in heat by certain outward signs such as a swollen vulva and bloody vaginal discharge. This is called the proestrus, and may last around 9 days. While she will not allow mating during this time, some manner of socialization between her and the sire may be conducted, at the very least to build a sense of familiarity between them.

The next period is the estrus, which also lasts approximately 9 days. The female is fertile during this time, and she will allow mating or breeding. Once breeding is successful, the typical practice is to have them mate every other day until she stops accepting the male. This is done to ensure a successful pregnancy. This is also why it is important to prepare beforehand suitable housing or accommodation for both dogs since they will be "living" together for some time during the breeding process. If you are breeding together dogs of different sizes, you should also be present during the process, to lend assistance if necessary.

Typically, the male will mount the female from the rear, and there will be rapid pelvic thrusts until ejaculation takes place. After this, the male will move around until they are rear to rear, but they will not separate for the next 10 to 30 minutes. This is known as the tie, and is natural. You should not try to separate them during this time because you might injure one or both of the dogs. They will separate naturally when they are ready.

The period of estrus is followed by the diestrus, which can last from 60 to 90 days. During this time, false pregnancy can sometimes happen, in which the dam shows all signs of being pregnant, even though she has not really conceived. The only way to confirm pregnancy is through an examination by your vet - either through abdominal palpitations ultrasound after 28 days.

Tips for Caring for your Pregnant Goldendoodle

The gestation period for dogs is usually 63 days, and you will need to take good care of pregnant dog during this time.

Once your vet confirms pregnancy, you might want to sit down and have a discussion with him regarding the best way of caring for your pregnant dog - this means adjustments in terms of your dog's regular exercise and diet, and if supplements may be required based on your dog's state of health. Pay attention to what your vet advises as this will be based on the unique circumstances of your dog.

Chapter Eight: Breeding Your Goldendoodle

In general, however, the following are some general guidelines you can follow as you care for and nurture your pregnant dam:

- Continue to provide your dog with regular, but not strenuous exercise. She needs to maintain her muscle tone and exercise keeps her from becoming overweight.
- If you haven't already, put her on a Premium dog food diet. This can supply her with all the necessary vitamins and minerals that she will need. Only give her supplements if your vet recommends it. Over-supplementing can be just as harmful - especially if you dog doesn't really need it.
- During the fourth or fifth week of pregnancy, you will gradually need to increase the frequency of her regular meals - until she is eating small meals every 3-4 hours during her last week of pregnancy. Many breeders choose to gradually change the mother's diet to premium performance or premium puppy food during this time, until she is completely on premium or puppy food during the last week of pregnancy. By this time, she should be eating 2-4 times the amount of her regular meals.
- There are some breeders that choose to add protein sources to the mother's diet, such as evaporated milk, eggs, meat or liver. These should never exceed more than 10 percent of her total meal, however. And

Chapter Eight: Breeding Your Goldendoodle

always remember to consult with your vet before you begin any dietary changes.

- Check her regularly for parasites such as fleas or ear mites, and bring her to the vet to check for internal parasites before birth. You don't want the puppies exposed almost immediately to these parasites soon after they are born.
- You should already have a whelping box prepared weeks before the whelping date. This box should be roomy enough to accommodate your dog and her expected brood, with low, raised sides if possible to prevent puppies from rolling out. Place this somewhere quiet and isolated to give her a sense of privacy. Try to get her accustomed to this box weeks before her whelping date, so that she will gravitate naturally towards this when she is near to giving birth. Otherwise, she might seek out some remote corner of your home to give birth. Many breeders begin to line the whelping box with newspapers before the due date as this is easy to clean and replace.
- Most importantly, be attentive and nurturing to your expectant mother. When she is nearing her whelping date, you might notice her becoming a bit more withdrawn and restless, or she may be seeking your attention more than usual. This can be a strange time for her - especially if she is a first-time mother.

Chapter Eight: Breeding Your Goldendoodle

Provide her with sufficient attention and security to help see her through this strange but exciting time.

Whelping Goldendoodle Puppies

There are a few signs you can watch out in your dog that will tell you that she is nearing her whelping date. A few days before she is due, you will notice a drop in appetite, and certain nesting behaviors. She will probably want to spend more time alone in her box.

Just before she will go into birth, her body temperature will drop from a normal 100 to 102.5 degrees to 99 degrees or lower. Expect her to go into labor within the next 24 hours.

The arrival of the puppies will be preceded signs of restlessness, and a dilated cervix. You will notice her beginning to pant or strain. There follows abdominal straining, and the puppies will start to be born.

Be on hand during this process - while most mothers will know what to do and can give birth easily without any intervention, some - especially first time mothers, might need a little assistance. Talk to her soothingly during this time, and reassure her with your presence. When the puppies, come out, they will each have their own placenta, and this must be removed so that the puppy can breathe. The mother will normally do this by herself, tearing the sac

Chapter Eight: Breeding Your Goldendoodle

with her teeth, chewing off the umbilical cord, and then licking each puppy to stimulate breathing. If she does not do this herself, or is unable to, then you will have to intervene. You can use sterilized scissors and unwaxed dental floss to cut the placenta and tie off the umbilical cord, using iodine for the cut ends to prevent infection. Then with the use of a moistened towel, carefully clean off the puppies' nose and mouth and to stimulate circulation so that they can start breathing.

You might not have to do this for all the puppies. Once the mother sees how it is done, she will naturally take over. The puppies will usually come at intervals of around ten minutes, sometimes more or less. Please make sure to count the placenta - each puppy should have its own.

It is important that the puppies are able to suckle from their mother as soon as possible. The mother's first milk, also known as colostrum, will provide them with much-needed antibodies while their own immune system is still developing. This maternal immunity will last for the first few days. Remember, however, that the puppies will only get antibodies for diseases that the mother has been vaccinated for.

You should have your veterinarian's number on hand during the whelping process in case things go wrong. Signs of trouble that warrant a call to a professional include:

Chapter Eight: Breeding Your Goldendoodle

- contractions for more than 45 minutes without any puppies being delivered
- signs that your mother is experiencing pain
- trembling, shivering, or collapse
- signs of a dark green or bloody fluid before the first puppy is born (this is normal only after the first puppy has been delivered)
- if there are still no signs of labor even after 64 days of pregnancy

Bring the mother to the veterinarian within 24 hours after her delivery for a checkup, and for the removal of any placentas which have been left inside her. She will be given an overall checkup to determine her state of health and her capacity for nursing her little ones. Consult with your vet at this time for how best to care for the mother and her newborns in the next coming weeks, particularly the dietary requirements for a lactating mother.

Caring for and Weaning the Puppies

Make sure to keep the puppies warm. Keep them away from drafts and chills. This entails proper regulation of the temperatures that the puppies are exposed to, as a chill, or overheating, can be detrimental to their health. Newly born puppies cannot regulate their body temperature during the first few weeks. If you provide them a heating

Chapter Eight: Breeding Your Goldendoodle

pad for instance, also provide them a cooler place in the box to which they can crawl to if they get too hot. Keep the temperatures at around 85 to 90 degrees for the first five days, after which you can gradually bring it down to 75 degrees by the end of the fourth week.

The dam should be fed at two or three times more than her normal diet for the next three weeks after whelping, as she will need the additional nourishment to provide milk for her puppies. Divide this into about three or four meals each day.

You can tell if the mother is providing adequate milk for her puppies from the state of the puppies themselves. A litter of plump and contented puppies means that the mother is providing them adequate nutrients through her milk. If you have thin and discontented puppies, you might want to bring the mother to a vet to figure out if she needs supplements.

Puppies have no other job than to feed, sleep, and keep warm. The mother will provide them with all that they need, though you should step at least in keeping their box clean by changing the soiled newspapers regularly.

Puppies grow quickly. Expect them to gain weight at a rate of 10-15% daily. At around three weeks, the puppies will begin to imitate their mother's feeding and drinking habits. Prepare for them a shallow water dish, and during 3 1/2 weeks, they can start receiving puppy mush.

Chapter Eight: Breeding Your Goldendoodle

Consult with your vet regarding the recommended food to start providing the puppies. Most opt for high quality dry puppy food moistened in puppy milk. Their intake will gradually increase as they are gradually weaned from nursing from their mother. By 7 weeks, they are ready for dry food. Ideally, they should be placed on the same puppy food that they were given in the beginning. At this time, once they are fully on a diet of dry food and drinking water, and the dam is able to leave them alone for long periods of time, they are fully weaned.

Once you begin giving your puppy moist food, you can also begin adjusting the mother's diet so that she can transition back to adult food and to help her decrease her milk production. By the 7th week, when the puppies are fully weaned, she should be back to eating adult food.

Be sure to introduce dietary changes gradually for both the puppies and their mother. Don't make any drastic changes to their diet, and introduce changes only with the approval and recommendation of your veterinarian.

Chapter Eight: Breeding Your Goldendoodle

Chapter Nine: Keeping Your Goldendoodle Healthy

Like most crossbreeds, the health of your Goldendoodle depends largely on the health of his parents. There are those who claim that crossbreeds are healthier than purebreds because of hybrid vigor, while there are those who also claim that this is just not true. Neither can be proven as an all-encompassing statement, however, because the health of each individual dog - whether crossbreed or purebred - still depends largely on their unique circumstances: their particular parentage, and how they were bred, raised, and their individual lifestyles. Even if you cross two different purebreds, if both parents suffer from one genetic condition or another, you'll get a

Chapter Nine: Keeping Your Goldendoodle Healthy

crossbreed puppy who might be prone to twice the genetic conditions.

It is therefore important for responsible breeders to go through the appropriate health checks for their breeding dogs before the actual breeding process - and for prospective owners to demand the appropriate documentation attesting to these health checks. This is all the more important these days, when designer dogs such as the Goldendoodles are so popular, and are demanding higher prices. It is a ripe field for the proliferation of puppy mills and breeders who breed irresponsibly and recklessly, driven only by monetary concerns rather than the welfare of their dogs and puppies.

While breeders may not be able to completely guarantee the health of her Goldendoodle puppies (there is no such thing as a 100% health guarantee), responsible breeders can do everything in their power to minimize the risk of genetic or inherited diseases among her puppies. Some of the health checks that Goldendoodle breeders may be expected to routinely secure for their breeding pairs include:

- hip certifications from the Orthopedic Foundation for Animals
- OFA heart clearance
- certification from the Canine Eye Registry Foundation

Chapter Nine: Keeping Your Goldendoodle Healthy

- OFA elbow clearance for standard sized Goldendoodles
- OFA knee clearance for small or medium-sized Goldendoodles
- DNA test for progressive retinal atrophy

More information regarding available health checks for Goldendoodles can be seen on the website of the Goldendoodle Association of North America (GANA), who have prescribed Red Ribbon and Blue Ribbon Accredited Breeder Health Testing Requirements. Please refer to the following resource:

GANA Accredited Breeder Health Testing Requirements
<http://www.goldendoodleassociation.com/health_testing.aspx>

Goldendoodles, like most dog breeds, can be prone to certain health conditions - in this case, the health conditions to which both Golden Retrievers and Poodles are prone to. While your Goldendoodle may not develop any of these conditions at all, it is always a good idea to be aware of them. Not only will you have a better idea of the potential lifestyle risks your Goldendoodle is prone to - being so forewarned can help you prevent or at least minimize the risks where appropriate. And if your Goldendoodle starts manifesting any telling symptoms, early diagnosis and treatment can also keep their condition from getting worse.

Chapter Nine: Keeping Your Goldendoodle Healthy

As with humans, early diagnosis and treatment is always best.

In the following section, we present you information regarding some of the more common conditions or illnesses that may affect Goldendoodles, the signs and symptoms of each, and the current state of treatments now available.

Common Health Problems Affecting Goldendoodles

Below are some of the common health problems that affect Goldendoodles. Please remember not to self-diagnose, or to treat your dog without professional medical advice. Should your Goldendoodle manifest any of the symptoms found below, bring them to a vet immediately.

Common Conditions Affecting Goldendoodles:

- Hip Dysplasia
- Elbow Dysplasia
- Hypothyroidism
- Von Willebrand's Disease
- Eye Conditions such as Juvenile-onset cataracts, Eyelid abnormalities (Entropion/Ectropion), Progressive Retinal Atrophy, Retinal , and Glaucoma
- Patellar Luxation

Chapter Nine: Keeping Your Goldendoodle Healthy

- Sebacious Adenitis
- Ear Infections
- Allergies
- Gastric Dilatation-Volvulus (Bloat)

Hip Dysplasia

Simply put, hip dysplasia is an inherited condition wherein the hip joints are improperly formed. Ideally, the hip mechanism is designed to move smoothly and freely, the ball rotating freely within the socket, and a connective tissue adding stability. In hip dysplasia, there is a laxity in the muscles and connective tissues, and joint laxity may develop. When the two bones within the joint lose contact with each other, subluxation develops. Subluxation can then affect the surrounding soft tissues and may even cause a drastic change in the size and shape of the articular surfaces of the joints.

It is important to know that most dogs that are prone to hip dysplasia actually start out with normal hips. The condition can manifest in all ages, but mainly during the middle or later years. If caught early, the condition can be managed so that the condition doesn't worsen with time - especially if your Goldendoodle is generally very active on a day-to-day basis.

Chapter Nine: Keeping Your Goldendoodle Healthy

Some of the symptoms to watch out for include a certain stiffness or soreness in the hips, a hesitancy or unwillingness to exercise, limping or bunny-hopping, pain or discomfort during or after exercise, resistance to fully extending the rear legs, difficulty climbing stairs, or walking or running with an altered gait. If your Goldendoodle starts manifesting any of these symptoms, bring them to your veterinarian immediately. Diagnosis is usually done through manual tests, physical examinations, and radiographs. This is generally not a difficult condition to diagnose, as the results are pretty straightforward.

Since hip dysplasia is a genetic condition, it cannot be completely prevented, though surgical hip replacement can be an option. Many times, however, treatment involves lifestyle changes such as modifying exercise requirements, maintaining regular weight, a prescribed diet, massage, and prescribed supplements and pain-relievers.

If your dog has been prescribed with hip dysplasia, avoid demanding or strenuous exercises, and make sure that your Goldendoodle is not exposed to cold or gets chilled. His sleeping area should be warm and dry. There are also those who consider swimming to be an excellent and therapeutic activity. And make sure that your pet's weight is kept within reasonable levels - being obese or overweight can place undue strain n your dog's legs and hips which may only worsen his condition.

Chapter Nine: Keeping Your Goldendoodle Healthy

Other things you can do for your dog include an orthopedic bed, and traction for slippery floors. Consult with your vet as you develop a treatment and management program that is just right for your dog.

Elbow Dysplasia

Elbow Dysplasia is similar, though a bit more complicated than hip dysplasia. There is abnormal growth in the cells, tissue or bone in the elbows, and this can manifest as any of four developmental abnormalities:

- Osteochondrosis - an abnormality in the cartilage and the bone underneath it
- Fragmentation of the medial coronoid process (FMCP) - the breaking up or degeneration of the bone in the ulna
- Ununited anconeal process (UAP) - where the anconeal process does not fuse with the ulna, resulting in joint instability when the humerus and ulna cannot function correctly together
- Elbow incongruity - where the radius and ulna do not grow at the same rate of speed, thus their surfaces cannot meet appropriately

Elbow dysplasia can manifest in a number of ways, including limping, holding out the leg from the body while walking, putting no weight on the leg, or even carrying the front leg completely. Your dog will certainly have a

Chapter Nine: Keeping Your Goldendoodle Healthy

diminished range of motion in the front legs, and flexing or extending the elbow can sometimes be painful.

It is necessary to get a proper diagnosis should your dog manifest any of the above symptoms, because oftentimes, it may not be elbow dysplasia at all. Your Vet can help you rule out any other possible causes such as trauma to the joint, an infection, a tumor, or an arthritic condition. X-rays and radiographs can help to confirm diagnosis.

The course of treatment will also have to depend on the findings during diagnosis - on which type of elbow dysplasia your dog has, and how far the condition has progressed. Many times, medical and therapeutic treatments can be prescribed for fragmented coronoid process and osteochondrosis - and a low-impact exercise program, coupled with medication to deal with pain and inflammation can work wonders.

On the other hand, surgery may be availed of in certain conditions - such as the removal of the fragmented process, or to treat the united anconeal process. Be sure to discuss your options carefully with your doctor, and don't hesitate to ask questions if there is anything that you don't understand. Be aware that while any course of treatment can help your dog to recover functionality and to decrease

Chapter Nine: Keeping Your Goldendoodle Healthy

the pain in his joints, degenerative joint disease or arthritis can be a long-term possibility regardless.

Hypothyroidism

Hypothyroidism should be of particular interest to the owners of Goldendoodles because of the many different dog breeds prone to this condition, Poodles and Golden Retrievers number among them. This also means an increased risk for Goldendoodles of getting hypothyroidism - a condition which is inherited.

Hypothyroidism happens when the thyroid gland does not produce enough thyroid hormones. The thyroid is part of the endocrine system, and is responsible for a variety of functions including controlling metabolism, regulating and synthesizing cholesterol, stimulating the growth of new red blood cells, the growth and development of our skeletal systems, and a multitude of other functions.

The presence of low or no thyroid hormones may be caused by deficiencies of the thyroid stimulating hormone, or it may be caused by autoimmune thyroiditis - when the immune system does not recognize the thyroid and attacks its cells. Either way, low thyroid hormones consequently affect the different functions of the thyroid, and can manifest in a variety of non-specific ways, such as:

- Lethargy
- Mental dullness

Chapter Nine: Keeping Your Goldendoodle Healthy

- Weight gain or obesity
- Cold intolerance
- High blood cholesterol
- Anemia
- Hyperpigmentation of the skin
- Dry hair or coat or excessive shedding
- Hair loss
- Mood swings and sudden behavioral changes such as anxiety, shyness or fearfulness, or aggression

If you notice your Goldendoodle manifesting any of the above symptoms, it may actually be due to a malfunctioning thyroid. Bring your dog to a vet immediately. Diagnosis is done through a blood test that checks the levels of thyroid hormones in your dog's system. Treatment generally consists of hormone replacements and thyroid medication.

If you suspect your Goldendoodle of suffering from hypothyroidism, try and raise it as a possibility with your vet if he doesn't raise it first. Given the rather generic range of symptoms - it's not an easy condition to catch from symptoms alone. The tragedy is that some owners opt to have their pets put down for sudden aggressive behavioral displays, when it could simply be a case of hypothyroidism - a condition which can improve dramatically given proper treatment and medication. If caught early, the prognosis is generally good. But if a dog lacks thyroid hormones for a

Chapter Nine: Keeping Your Goldendoodle Healthy

prolonged period of time, their outlook may not be so favorable.

Von Willebrand's Disease

VWD is the most common hereditary blood clotting disorder among dogs, and it occurs with more frequency in certain breeds, including standard Poodles, and Golden Retrievers. This means that it is also just as likely to affect Goldendoodles.

VWD is caused by the deficiency of the von Willebrand Factor (vWF) in the blood. This is an adhesive glycoprotein that helps blood clotting. The lack of it can lead to excessive bleeding in certain instances, such as after an injury.

Symptoms to watch out for include:

- Nosebleeds
- Blood in the stool
- Blood in the urine
- Bleeding gums
- Excessive bleeding from the vagina
- Anemia
- Prolonged bleeding after surgery, trauma, or after an injury
- Skin bruising

Chapter Nine: Keeping Your Goldendoodle Healthy

Diagnosis is done through the buccal mucosal bleeding time (BMBT), which measures the length of time that it takes platelets to plug a small injury. Together with other tests such as a blood chemical profile, urinalysis, blood count, and a blood test to measure the exact amount of von Willebrand factor present in the blood can confirm diagnosis of VWD.

In cases of severe blood loss, transfusion may help to stabilize the patient. There are also certain medications that has been said to raise the levels of von Willebrand Factor in the blood, but so far, there are no definite scientific results. Discuss your options with your vet, and discuss also the kind of lifestyle your dog can live to avoid precipitating this condition. Most dogs can still lead a good and healthy life even with VWD, though you will have to take care to avoid certain triggers that may increase the risk of bleeding. Stress, for instance, should be avoided, and you should also exercise appropriate caution if your dog should suffer from any minor injuries.

Eye Conditions

Goldendoodles may be prone to suffer from certain eye conditions, including any of the following:

Juvenile-onset cataracts

Poodles as a breed have been known to be prone to Juvenile Cataracts, and because this is an inherited

Chapter Nine: Keeping Your Goldendoodle Healthy

condition, Goldendoodles are also similarly prone, though external factors such as trauma, progressive retinal atrophy, and other injuries may also cause cataracts. Juvenile cataracts can occur from between 6 months to 6 years of age.

This is different from old-age cataracts, which does not seem to bear any relationship to the incidence of juvenile cataracts. Juvenile cataracts are either dissolving or total and irreversible. In dissolving cataracts, vision can be restored through the use of cortisone drops. On the other hand, surgery is the only viable option for the non-dissolving type.

The onset of cataracts among young dogs is usually quick and intense - occurring from between 24 to 72 hours. If you notice any changes in the colors or the clarity of your puppy's eyes, or if you notice him squinting or scratching at his eyes, bring him to a vet immediately. Other possible signs include bumping into furniture, or if you notice a whitish spot in their eyes.

Eyelid abnormalities (Entropion/Ectropion)

There are two possible eyelid abnormalities which your pet may suffer from - these are conformational abnormalities that may cause your pet's eyes to roll inward or outward. Respectively, these are referred to as Entropion and Ectropion.

Entropion is the inward rolling of the eyelids. This can occur in both the upper and lower eyelids, though more

Chapter Nine: Keeping Your Goldendoodle Healthy

commonly in the latter. When this happens, the eyelashes rub against the surface of the eye, which can cause irritation. If the eye suffers from prolonged irritation of this kind, it may lead to scratches or ulceration of the cornea, increased tear production, conjunctivitis, and to the formation of a thick, yellow discharge. Sometimes, there can be perforation, and dark scar tissues can form over the wound, called pigmentary keratitis. Altogether, this can lead to decrease or loss of vision.

In young puppies, a temporary suture can be used to place the lids into normal position, and this protects the puppy's eyes while he is growing. If all goes well, this can actually address the condition permanently. If not, surgery is usually recommended. For the secondary problems, artificial tears can be used to lubricate the eyes, and ulcerated corneas are treated with antibiotics. Routine medical follow-up is important, as procedures may need to be repeated until the problem is resolved.

Ectropion, on the other hand, is the outward rolling of the eyelids. Though sometimes considered desirable in some dog breeds - the droopy-eyed look is seen as endearing by many - it is not really healthy for your pet's eyes. It may lead to excessive tear production which are not well distributed over the surface of the eye. As a result, dry eye can occur. Ectropion may also lead to redness and inflammation of the conjunctiva.

Chapter Nine: Keeping Your Goldendoodle Healthy

Most cases of ectropion are mild, and require no intervention other than topical drops or ointments when warranted. In severe cases, however, surgery is recommended in order to prevent ongoing ocular disease.

Progressive Retinal Atrophy

In Progressive Retinal Atrophy (PRA), the retinal tissue atrophies or degenerates. This is a slowly progressing disease, so the early signs may easily be overlooked. It is comparable to a slowly dimming light within a room. Precisely because of this very slow progression, the eyes adapt to the changes and the gradual loss of vision is not noticed until the dog is nearly blind.

While the symptoms may not be very noticeable, they can include any of the following:

- Night blindness which can gradually progress to day blindness. In this case, your dog may show some hesitancy or fear in going outside when it is dark. They will stay close to sources of light, and may even be hesitant in wandering inside the house when it is night.
- There is a characteristic shine from the eyes
- Dilated pupils and/or slow response to light
- The formation of cataracts as secondary to PRA, generally during the later stages of the disease

Chapter Nine: Keeping Your Goldendoodle Healthy

An ophthalmic examination can diagnose the existence of PRA, or through an electroretinography test. Unfortunately, being an inherited condition, there is no cure for PRA. This is another instance why eye checks and screening is so important prior to breeding.

Retinal Dysplasia

Retinal Dysplasia is another inherited condition which may result in round clumps or "rosettes" or "folds" in the retinal tissue. Sometimes, it may also be caused by external factors such as trauma.

There is no treatment for Retinal Dysplasia. The effects can range among a variety of vision problems, from small blind spots to total blindness. While vision can be affected, it is usually not painful or progressive. Many dogs can still live long and full lives even with this condition, as they adapt and their senses compensate greatly for the resulting loss or diminished vision. At its most severe form, however, complete retinal dysplasia may lead to blindness and may even be accompanied by secondary eye problems such as cataracts or glaucoma.

Glaucoma

Glaucoma is quite common among certain dog breeds, and this happens when there is high intraocular pressure inside the eye due to the lack of sufficient drainage of a liquid called aqueous humor. When the fluid builds up,

Chapter Nine: Keeping Your Goldendoodle Healthy

the pressure rises, and this can crush or displace the eye's internal structures such as the retina and the optic nerve.

Glaucoma can either be primary or secondary. It is primary when it is genetic, and secondary when it is caused by or secondary to other conditions such as trauma or injury, infections or inflammations. In either case, quick action is essential. Treatment is generally geared to relieving these conditions, consisting of reducing the pressure within the eye, reducing the amount of fluid buildup, increasing drainage, and when necessary, pain relief. If this condition is not addressed quickly, the effects may be irreversible.

Watch out for the following symptoms:

- dilated pupils
- cloudiness within the cornea
- increased size in the vessels of the eyes
- a larger or protruding eye compared to the other
- indications of pain such as when the dog rubs at his eyes with his paw, or fluttering or squinting the eyes
- redness or bloodshot eyes

A case of glaucoma is properly considered an emergency case, and it is essential that you bring your dog to your vet immediately.

Patellar Luxation

A Luxating Patella is more commonly seen among smaller or toy dog breeds. Normally, the patella or knee cap slides along a deep groove in the femur or thigh bone. But when the groove is too shallow, due to either trauma or malformation, the patella luxates, or jump out of the groove and moves sideways - typically towards the inside of the leg.

In short, luxating patella happens when the kneecap slips or is dislocated from its original or normal position. This causes the leg to "lock up" - most dogs will usually hold the foot off the ground for a while - sometimes for a few hours, sometimes for several days. This is because the patella cannot return to its normal position until after the muscles of the quadriceps relax and lengthens.

This can happen intermittently, and while you might often hear your dog yip in pain for a short while, you'll notice him using his rear legs normally after a while as if nothing had happened. But untreated, it can happen intermittently over a period of time, causing unnecessary wear and tear in the knee joints. Eventually, this may lead to arthritis or a permanently swollen knee.

While not always necessary, the main treatment for this condition is surgical. Preferably, however, dogs diagnosed with a luxating patella should not be bred to prevent this condition from being passed down to their offspring.

Sebacious Adenitis

Sebaceous Adenitis is a relatively uncommon condition among dogs, but which a Goldendoodle may inherit from its Poodle parent or grandparent. This affects the sebacious glands in the skin, which may become inflamed and are eventually destroyed.

Diagnosis of this condition is through a skin biopsy, but even the initial symptoms can be telling:

- whitish scaling in the skin
- waxy, matted hair
- sparse or dull fur
- hair loss
- lesions in the skin
- itching may take place once infection has set in

The signs tend to affect first the areas of the head, neck and back, spreading downward and backward.

Because this condition is inherited, there is no cure, but it can be managed, usually with frequent shampooing and the administration of antimicrobial treatments. Sometimes, your vet may prescribe fatty acid supplements to replace the sebum that the sebaceous glands normally

Chapter Nine: Keeping Your Goldendoodle Healthy

produce. As in most inherited conditions, it is best if those diagnosed with this condition are not bred to begin with.

Ear Infections

The long, low hanging ears of Goldendoodles are part of their unique charm, but it can also be the cause of certain problems. Because of the abundance of hair covering these long-hanging ear flaps, it can be also be a perfect site for infections. And because many Goldendoodles are fond of the water and of swimming, moisture can be trapped within these ears, and when they cannot dry properly, bacteria can set in.

It has been noticed by some that Goldendoodles with curly coat hair seem to be the most prone to ear infections. Multiple hairs cover the ears, and there are also hairs that grow deep within the ear canal. These hairs trap moisture, which can cause yeast infection. Sometimes, ear infections can be caused by ear mites - recognizable for their foul smell.

Regular ear cleaning should be a regular part of your grooming sessions. Sometimes though, ear infections can set in despite our best efforts. You might notice your Goldendoodle tilting his head to one side, shaking his head, scratching or pawing at his ear, or you may notice a certain smell coming from within the ears, coupled with a dark or yellowish discharge. If you do notice any of these

Chapter Nine: Keeping Your Goldendoodle Healthy

symptoms, bring your dog to the vet for proper diagnosis before appropriate treatment can be prescribed.

Always remember to be careful when you are cleaning, treating, or even just observing the insides of your pet's ears - sometimes ear infections can even be precipitated by improper ear cleaning methods. Please remember that the insides of a dog's ears are very sensitive, and must be handled with care. It is best to have a professional examine your pet's ears if you notice something wrong. Proper diagnosis is also important as improper treatments may only exacerbate their condition.

Allergies

Dogs can suffer from allergies just as humans, and the causes are just as diverse. Some of the more common things that dogs can be allergic to include dust mites, pollen, mold, and fleas. Some may also suffer from food allergies, or be allergic to certain substances or ingredients.

Allergies are usually caused by an overactive immune system that views what are generally non-harmful substances as threats. Allergic reactions can span the gamut of itchiness, rashes, itchy eyes, sneezing, or even vomiting. More often than not, however, itchiness is the primary symptom, which often affect the areas of the face, ears, belly, feet, and the armpit region.

Chapter Nine: Keeping Your Goldendoodle Healthy

There are some medications that can help with allergies, and some vets may prescribe specific shampoo or rinses that help alleviate the itchiness. What is important, however, is to identify the allergen and to eliminate it from the dog's immediate environment.

Gastric Dilatation-Volvulus

Gastric Dilatation-Volvulus is the more technical or scientific term for bloating. This is a life-threatening condition for dogs, and can progress rapidly once it starts. Some dogs have been known to die within several hours after bloating.

Some veterinarians also refer to this as stomach torsion or twisted stomach. For a variety of reasons, when the stomach fills up with air, this results in undue pressure on the diaphragm and other internal organs. Aside from making it difficult for the dog to breathe, the compression of large veins in the abdomen can also prevent blood from traveling to the heart. The stomach can literally rotate, cutting off blood supply, at which point the dog's condition rapidly worsens.

This is a serious and life-threatening condition, and some breeds do seem to be more susceptible than others, including the Standard Poodle. It also seems to have genetic factors, so a predisposition to this condition may be passed on to the dog's offspring. It affects males more commonly

Chapter Nine: Keeping Your Goldendoodle Healthy

than females, and the risk can apparently be increased by nervous or anxious temperaments, and even eating habits (i.e., dogs who eat rapidly if fed only once a day, or those that exercise soon after meals).

Symptoms include the most obvious sign of bloating which is a swollen or distended abdomen. The dog may also retch, or try to vomit without anything coming out, or may display signs of profuse salivation, rapid shallow breathing, and abdominal pain.

Owners of dog breeds that are prone to or susceptible to bloat should be aware of the signs, and be ready to act quickly should symptoms begin to show. Treatment generally consists of releasing the gas from the stomach, whether through a tube or the insertion of a large needle. The condition must be monitored closely after treatment, to detect possible heart arrhythmias, blood clots, or signs of infection. Once the dog's condition is stabilized, surgery may be used to reposition the stomach and prevent a recurrence of the stomach twisting again.

Preventing Illness with Vaccinations

While Goldendoodles do seem to be prone to a great number of congenital conditions, these are usually

Chapter Nine: Keeping Your Goldendoodle Healthy

addressed by proper and responsible breeding processes and protocols. Doing so greatly minimizes the risk that your dog may have inherited one condition or another.

And yet another way of safeguarding your Goldendoodle's health is by vaccines. Congenital conditions aside, there are also certain contagious and life-threatening diseases that afflict the canine population, and up-to-date vaccinations can protect your pet from contracting any of them. This is true even if your dog is mostly kept indoors.

Vaccines work by preparing the body's immune system to fight off certain diseases or organisms. Should your pet ever be exposed to the actual disease, his immune system recognizes it and is prepared to defend against it.

Nowadays, vaccines are divided into core and non-core. While non-core vaccines are not universally required and may only be administered if there is a greater risk based on several factors such as your dog's lifestyle and the prevailing conditions in your region, core vaccines are considered mandatory.

Core vaccines include those for Distemper, Parainfluenza and Parvovirus (DHPP), and Rabies. Non-core vaccines are those for Leptospirosis, Bordetella (Kennel Cough), Lyme Disease, Canine Influenza, and Corona Virus.

Below is a table providing a general guideline for the vaccination schedule of dogs. This may be adjusted,

Chapter Nine: Keeping Your Goldendoodle Healthy

however, depending on your Goldendoodle's physical condition and the recommendations of your vet:

Age	Vaccination
5 weeks	Parvovirus
6 and 9 weeks	Combination vaccine (for adenovirus, hepatitis, distemper, parainfluenza, and parvovirus); also coronavirus and leptospirosis when necessary in the region
12 weeks	Rabies
12-16 weeks	Combination vaccine (for adenovirus, hepatitis, distemper, parainfluenza, and parvovirus); also coronavirus, leptospirosis, and lyme disease
Boosters	Combination vaccine (for adenovirus, hepatitis, distemper, parainfluenza, and parvovirus); also coronavirus, lyme disease, and rabies

Chapter Nine: Keeping Your Goldendoodle Healthy

For booster shots, the only required vaccination is for rabies, although the regional conditions in your area may require additional booster shots for other vaccines. If you are concerned about the possible deleterious effects of too much or too frequent vaccinations, don't hesitate to raise your concerns with your vet and discuss your options.

Goldendoodle Care Sheet

This section contains a summary of many of the important points regarding the Goldendoodle breed that has been presented to you within this book. It is a quick reference guide that you can easily look through or refer to whenever you are seeking specific information or details but have no time to go through the body of this book. It will also give you a good overview of the Goldendoodle breed, as you try to determine whether or not this is the right breed for you.

1.) Basic Goldendoodle Information

Pedigree: Golden Retriever, Poodle

AKC Group: not applicable; this is a relatively new breed that is not yet recognized by any of the international dog organizations

Types: no distinctions as to type

Breed Size: can range from standard, medium, and miniature

Height: for Standard Goldendoodles, height is at 22-26 inches tall at the withers; mini Goldendoodles have an average height of from 10-15 inches tall at the withers

Weight: Standard Goldendoodles can weigh from 50 to 90 lbs.; mini Goldendoodles weigh from 10 to 30 lbs

Coat: can be either wavy or curly, and may be (but not always) hypoallergenic and non-shedding; coats can resemble either of their parents' coats

Coat Color: variety of colors, including apricot, red, gold, black, silver, blue, chocolate, fawn, white, or parti-colored

Eyes: eyes are almond-shaped and can range in colors from brown, green, blue and amber;

Ears: can vary from long, heavy hanging ears or shorter ears that flip over the top

Temperament: friendly, loving, gentle, playful, trusting, naturally intelligent and biddable, and eager to please

Strangers: are friendly with strangers, do not make good guard dogs; toy Goldendoodles may not be stranger-friendly

Other Dogs: provided proper introduction and socialization, generally get along well with other dogs

Other Pets: provided proper introduction and socialization, get along well with other pets

Training: highly intelligent and easy to train; responds well to positive reinforcement

Exercise Needs: regular, moderate exercise and periods of play

Health Conditions: Hip Dysplasia, Elbow Dysplasia, Hypothyroidism, Von Willebrand's Disease, Eye Conditions (such as Juvenile-onset cataracts, Eyelid abnormalities [Entropion/Ectropion], Progressive Retinal Atrophy, and Glaucoma), Patellar Luxation, Sebacious Adenitis, Ear Infections, Allergies, and Gastric Dilatation-Volvulus (Bloat)

Lifespan: average 10 to 15 years

2.) *Habitat Requirements*

Recommended Accessories: crate, dog bed, food/water dishes, treats, toys, collar, leash, identification tag, harness, grooming supplies

Collar and Harness: sized by weight

Grooming Supplies: brush, shampoo, toenail clippers

Grooming Frequency: depends on the coat type; at least a weekly brushing, and professional grooming every 4-6 weeks

Energy Level: active and energetic, requiring a fair amount of exercise every day

Exercise Requirements: half an hour to an hour of playing or walking each day

Crate: highly recommended

Crate Size: just large enough for dog to lie down and turn around comfortably

Crate Extras: lined with blanket or plush pet bed

Food/Water: stainless steel or ceramic bowls, clean daily

Toys: start with an assortment, see what the dog likes; include some mentally stimulating toys

Exercise Ideas: walking, retrieval games, playing ball, swimming

3.) Nutritional Needs

Nutritional Needs: water, protein, carbohydrate, fats, vitamins, minerals

RER: 30 (body weight in kilograms) + 70

Calorie Needs: varies by age, weight, and activity level; RER modified with activity level

Amount to Feed (puppy): 4 meals a day, reducing to 3 meals a day after 3 months, and 3 meals after six months, at regular intervals

Amount to Feed (adult): consult recommendations on the package; calculated by weight

Important Ingredients: fresh animal protein (chicken, beef, lamb, turkey, eggs), digestible carbohydrates (rice, oats, barley), animal fats

Important Minerals: calcium, phosphorus, potassium, magnesium, iron, copper and manganese

Important Vitamins: Vitamin A, Vitamin A, Vitamin B-12, Vitamin D, Vitamin C

Look For: AAFCO statement of nutritional adequacy; protein at top of ingredients list; no artificial flavors, dyes, preservatives

4.) Breeding Information

Age of First Heat: around 6 months to two years old

Heat (Estrus) Cycle: 14 to 21 days

Frequency: twice a year, every 6 to 7 months

Greatest Fertility: 11 to 15 days into the cycle

Gestation Period: 59 to 63 days

Pregnancy Detection: possible after 21 days, best to wait 28-30 days before exam

Feeding Pregnant Dogs: maintain normal diet until week 5 or 6 then slightly increase rations by 20 to 50 percent for the last five weeks

Signs of Labor: body temperature drops below normal 100° to 102°F (37.7° to 38.8°C), may be as low as 98°F (36.6°C); dog begins nesting in a dark, quiet place

Contractions: ten to thirty minutes, in waves of an hour or so each time

Whelping: may last anywhere from a few hours to half a day or more

Puppies: born with eyes and ears closed; eyes open at 3 weeks, teeth develop at 10 weeks

Litter Size: average 3 to 8 puppies

Size at Birth: varies depending on size, whether miniature, medium, or standard size Goldendoodle

Weaning: supplement with controlled portions of moistened puppy food at 3-5 weeks, with water freely available, fully weaned at 5-6 weeks

Socialization: start as early as possible to prevent puppies from being nervous as an adult, preferably before 14-16 weeks of age

Index

A

AAFCO	124
Age of First Heat	124
Alcohol	54
Allergies	7, 14, 97, 113, 121, 152, 153
Apple seeds	54
Avocado	55

B

bathing	6, 70, 71
Bleeding gums	103
bloat	115
Blood in the stool	103
Blood in the urine	103
Breed Size	13, 120
breeders	5, 29
breeding	5, 6, 7, 77, 78, 82
Brushing Teeth	72

C

Calorie Needs	123
Carbohydrates	6, 47, 123
cataracts	107
Cherry pits	55
Chocolate	55
choosing a puppy	32, 33
Citrus	55
Cleaning Ears	7, 75
Clipper blades	69
cloudiness within the cornea	109
coat	3, 4, 5, 7, 13, 67, 68, 120

Coconut	55
Coffee	55
Cold intolerance	102
Collar and Harness	42, 122
costs	21, 22, 23, 25
Crate	42, 122
crate training	59, 62, 63

D

Daily Energy Requirements	6, 48, 50
Dangerous Foods	6, 53, 54
dilated pupils	107, 109
dog food	52, 53, 123, 124
Dry hair or coat or excessive shedding	102

E

Ear Infections	7, 14, 97, 112, 121, 154
ears	4, 13, 120, 125
ectropion	107
Elbow Dysplasia	7, 14, 96, 99, 121, 155
Elbow incongruity	99
Energy Level	122
Exercise	14, 43, 44, 121, 122, 123
Eye Conditions	7, 14, 96, 104, 121
Eyelid abnormalities (Entropion/Ectropion)	105
eyes	3, 120, 125

F

Fats	6, 48, 123
food	7, 122
Food and water bowls	42, 122

G

Garlic	55
Gastric Dilatation-Volvulus	7, 14, 97, 114, 121
Glaucoma	14, 108, 109, 121, 155, 156
Glossary	5, 2
Grapes/raisins	55
Greatest Fertility	124
grooming	5, 25, 67, 68, 69, 71, 72, 122
Grooming supplies	42, 122

H

hair	2, 3, 4, 6
hair loss	102, 111
harness	122
Health Conditions	14, 93, 96, 121
Heat	5, 124
Height	13, 120
High blood cholesterol	102
hip certifications	94
Hip Dysplasia	7, 5, 14, 96, 97, 121, 157
history	14
Hops	55
house	3, 4
Housebreaking	6, 61, 67
Hyperpigmentation of the skin	102
Hypothyroidism	7, 14, 96, 101, 121, 157, 159

I

Ideal Habitat Requirements	6, 40
increased size in the vessels of the eyes	109
Initial Costs	22

J

Juvenile-onset cataracts	14, 104, 121

K

kennel	4, 5

L

leash	5, 42, 122
lesions in the skin	111
Lethargy	101
license	5
Lifespan	14, 121
Litter Size	125
luxating patella	110

M

Macadamia nuts	55
Mental dullness	101
milk	7, 55
Mold	55
Mood swings	102
Mushrooms	55
Mustard seeds	55

N

Nail Clippers	69
Neuter	5
Nosebleeds	103
Nutritional Needs	6, 45, 46, 47, 50, 90, 91, 123, 124

O

OFA elbow clearance	95
OFA heart clearance	94
OFA knee clearance	95
Onions/leeks	55

Osteochondrosis	99
Other Dogs	14, 121
Other Pets	14, 21, 121

P

paper training	62
Parvovirus	117, 125
Patellar Luxation	7, 14, 96, 109, 121
Peach pits	55
Pedigree	6, 12, 120
Pin Brush	69
Positive Reinforcement Training	6, 64
Potato leaves/stems	55
Pregnancy	84, 85, 86, 87, 89, 124
Progressive Retinal Atrophy	14, 107, 121, 160
pros and cons	5, 23, 25
protein	6, 47, 123, 124
puppies	5, 7, 8, 90, 123, 125
Puppy-Proofing	5, 35, 36, 160
purchasing	5, 27, 28

R

Rabies	117
Raw meat and eggs	55
Recommended Tools	6, 69
redness or bloodshot eyes	109
regular trips outdoors	62
RER	49, 50, 123
rescues	28, 29
Retinal Dysplasia	108, 160
Rhubarb leaves	55

S

Salty snacks	55
Sebacious Adenitis	7, 14, 97, 111, 121
Size at Birth	125
Skin bruising	103
Slicker brush	69
Socialization	6, 59, 125
Strangers	14, 121
supplies	6, 41, 42, 69, 122

T

Tea	55
teeth	3, 125
Temperament	13, 16, 24, 43, 44, 121
temperature	124
Tomato leaves/stems	55
Toxic or harmful plants	35
toys	42, 122
Training	14, 57, 121
trembling, shivering, or collapse	89
Trimming Nails	7, 74

U

undercoat	3, 7
undercoat rake	122
Ununited anconeal process (UAP)	99

V

Vaccination	115, 116, 117, 124
Vitamins and Minerals	6, 48, 123
Von Willebrand's Disease	7, 14, 96, 103, 121, 162

W

Walnuts	55
water	42, 47, 122, 123
waxy, matted hair	111
Weaning	7, 89, 125
weight	13, 120, 122, 123
Weight gain or obesity	102
Whelping	7, 87, 88, 89, 124, 125
Whiskers	7, 8
whitish scaling in the skin	111

X

Xylitol	55

Y

Yeast dough	55

Photo Credits

Page 1 Photo by lyrandian via Wikimedia Commons as uploaded by Pharaoh Hound.
<https://commons.wikimedia.org/wiki/File:Goldendoodle_standing.jpg>

Page 9 Photo by Raduw at the English language Wikipedia via Wikimedia Commons.
<https://commons.wikimedia.org/wiki/File:Goldendoodle_puppy.jpg>

Page 17 Photo by William Warby via Wikimedia Commons.
<https://commons.wikimedia.org/wiki/File:Goldendoodle_puppy_Marty.jpg>

Page 27 Photo by brookelstone via Pixabay.
<https://pixabay.com/en/goldendoodle-puppy-two-months-1234760/>

Page 39 Photo by Godsgirl via Pixabay.
<https://pixabay.com/en/goldendoodle-dog-canine-pet-animal-750444/>

Page 45 Photo by DanielBrachlow via Pixabay.
<https://pixabay.com/en/dog-sea-dog-on-beach-play-hybrid-1242909/>

Page 57 Photo by Kaz via Pixabay.
<https://pixabay.com/en/goldendoodle-dog-happy-running-164935/>

Page 67 Photo by Daniel X. O'Neil via Flickr.
<https://www.flickr.com/photos/juggernautco/6298878700/>

Page 77 Photo by Mary Anne Morgan via Flickr.
<https://www.flickr.com/photos/maryannemorgan/25001306610/>

Page 93 Photo by Andrea Arden via Flickr.
<https://www.flickr.com/photos/andrea_arden/8340976526/>

Page 119 Photo by Sonny Abesamis via Flickr.
<https://www.flickr.com/photos/enerva/5446794511/>

References

"8 Must-Have Puppy Products." Wendy Wilson. <https://www.cesarsway.com/dog-care/puppy/8-must-have-puppy-products-for-you>

"A Doodle Is As A Doodle Does." Catster. <http://www.catster.com/cats/205658/diary/A_doodle_is_a s_a_doodle_does/320971>

"A Stress-Free Way for Trimming Your Dog's Toenails." Dr. Karen Gellman. <http://www.dogsnaturallymagazine.com/trimming-your-dogs-toenails/>

"Abnormal Development of the Elbow in Dogs." PetMD. <http://www.petmd.com/dog/conditions/musculoskeletal/c _dg_elbow_dysplasia#>

"Abnormal Eyelid in Dogs." PetMD. <http://www.petmd.com/dog/conditions/eyes/c_multi_entr opion#>

"About Goldendoodles." About Goldendoodles. <http://f1bdoodles.com/rich_text_2.html>

"Accredited Breeder Health Testing Requirements." GANA. <http://www.goldendoodleassociation.com/health_testing. aspx>

"Allergies in Dogs." WebMD. <http://pets.webmd.com/dogs/allergies-dogs>

"Allergies: What You Need To Know." Henry Cenry, DVM, MS. <https://www.cesarsway.com/dog-care/allergies/allergies-what-you-need-to-know>

"Are Doodle Dogs Worth Their Price?" Reuters. <http://www.reuters.com/article/us-expensive-dogs-idUSTRE81829320120209>

"Bleeding Disorder in Dogs." PetMD. <http://www.petmd.com/dog/conditions/cardiovascular/c_dg_von_willebrand_disease>

"Bloat (Gastric Dilatation and Volvulus) in Dogs." Pet Education. <http://www.peteducation.com/article.cfm?c=2+2090&aid=402>

"Breeding for Dog Owners - Caring for Newborn Puppies." VCA. <http://www.vcahospitals.com/main/pet-health-information/article/animal-health/breeding-for-dog-owners-caring-for-newborn-puppies/488>

"Canine Nutrition Basics." Claudia Kawczynska. <http://thebark.com/content/canine-nutrition-basics>

"Caring for a Newborn Puppy." WebMD. <http://pets.webmd.com/dogs/guide/caring-newborn-puppy>

"Caring for Newborn Puppies & Their Mother." Pet Education. <http://www.peteducation.com/article.cfm?c=2+2108&aid=916>

"Designer Dogs." The Kennel Club. <http://www.thekennelclub.org.uk/our-resources/media-centre/issue-statements/designer-dogs/>

"Designer Dogs (Hybrid Dogs)." Dog Breed Info Center. <http://www.dogbreedinfo.com/designerdogs.htm>

"Do I Need to Brush My Dog's Teeth?" Banfield Pet Hospital. <http://www.banfield.com/pet-health-resources/preventive-care/dental/do-i-need-to-brush-my-dog-s-teeth>

"Does your Goldendoodle have an ear infection?" Goldendoodle World. <http://www.articlesbase.com/pets-articles/does-your-goldendoodle-have-an-ear-infection-870312.html>

"Dog Ear Infections. Gorgeous Doodles. <http://gorgeousdoodles.com/helpful-labradoodle-information/dog-care-library/dog-ear-infections/>

"Dog Nutrition Tips." ASPCA. <http://www.aspca.org/pet-care/dog-care/dog-nutrition-tips>

"Dogs: Positive Reinforcemenet Training." The Humane Society of the United States.

<http://www.humanesociety.org/animals/dogs/tips/dog_training_positive_reinforcement.html>

"Doodle and Poodle Ear Care." Dreamydoodles. <http://www.dreamydoodles.com/doodle-and-poodle-ear-care/>

"Doodle Breed History." Goldendoodle &Labradoodle. <http://www.goldendoodle-labradoodle.org/doodle-info/goldendoodle-labradoodle-breed-history/>

"Doodle Health Issues." Goldendoodles and Labradoodles. <http://www.goldendoodle-labradoodle.org/doodle-info/goldendoodle-labradoodle-breed-health-issues/>

"Ectropion in Dogs: What's Wrong With My Dog's Eyes?" Dr. Mike Paul, DVM. <http://www.pethealthnetwork.com/dog-health/dog-diseases-conditions-a-z/ectropion-dogs-whats-wrong-my-dogs-eyes>

"Elbow Dysplasia." Drs. Foster & Smith, Inc. <http://www.peteducation.com/article.cfm?c=2+2084&aid=431>

"FAQ: Goldendoodles." Goldendoodles. <http://goldendoodles.com/faqs/goldendoodle_faq.htm>

"FAQs Section." Goldendoodles. <http://goldendoodles.com/faqs/goldendoodle_faq.htm>

"Glaucoma in Dogs." PetMD. <http://www.petmd.com/dog/conditions/eyes/c_dg_glaucoma>

"Glaucoma in Dogs: An Eye Emergency." Race Foster, DVM. <http://www.peteducation.com/article.cfm?c=2+2092&aid=439>

"Goldendoodle." Great Breeds. <http://greatbreeds.com/articles/goldendoodle.html>

"Goldendoodle." Pet Guide. <http://www.petguide.com/breeds/dog/goldendoodle/>

"Goldendoodle." Purina. <http://www.purina.com.au/owning-a-dog/dog-breeds/Goldendoodle>

"Goldendoodle." VetStreet. <http://www.vetstreet.com/dogs/goldendoodle#health>

"Goldendoodle." Wikipedia. <https://en.wikipedia.org/wiki/Goldendoodle>

"Goldendoodle Grooming Tools: What You Need for a Successful Groom." All About Goldendoodle Grooming. <http://www.goldendoodlegrooming.com/goldendoodle-grooming-tools/>

"Goldendoodle - Temperament & Personality." PetWave. <http://www.petwave.com/Dogs/Breeds/Goldendoodle/Temperament.aspx>

"Goldendoodles 101: History and Personality." Everything Doodle. <http://www.everythingdoodle.com/goldendoodle-101-history-personality/>

"Goldendoodles on Trial." MuttPuppies on Trial. <http://muttpuppiesontrial.blogspot.com/2008/09/goldendoodles-on-trial.html>

"Grooming Your Goldendoodle." Bev LaLonde. <http://goldendoodles.com/groom/groomingdoods.htm>

"Hair Types & Grooming for a Goldendoodle." Bethany Seeley. <https://www.cuteness.com/article/hair-types-grooming-goldendoodle>

"Help for Canines with Hypothyroidism." Shannon Wilkinson. <http://www.whole-dog-journal.com/issues/8_6/features/Dogs-With-Hypothyroidism_15723-1.html>

"Hip Dysplasia in Dogs." ASPCA. <http://pets.webmd.com/dogs/canine-hip-dysplasia>

"Hip Dysplasia in Dogs: Diagnosis, Treatment, and Prevention." Veterinary & Aquatic Services Department, Drs. Foster & Smith. <http://www.peteducation.com/article.cfm?c=2+2084&aid=444>

"History of the Goldendoodle." Goldendoodle Association of North America."
<http://www.goldendoodleassociation.com/history.aspx>

"How Much to Feed a Dog to Meet His Energy Needs." Pet Education.
<http://www.peteducation.com/article.cfm?c=2+1659&aid=2612>

"How to Care for Newborn Puppies." Ashley Bennett.
<https://www.cesarsway.com/dog-care/puppies/how-to-care-for-newborn-puppies>

"How to Choose a Good Puppy (Picking the Best Puppy in a Litter)." Michele Welton.
<http://www.yourpurebredpuppy.com/buying/articles/how-to-choose-a-puppy.html>

"How to Find a Good Dog Breeder." Gwen Bailey.
<http://www.apbc.org.uk/articles/good_breeder>

"How to Find a Responsible Dog Breeder." The Humane Society of the United States.
<http://www.humanesociety.org/issues/puppy_mills/tips/finding_responsible_dog_breeder.html>

"How to Groom a Goldendoodle: a Step-by-Step Guide." All About Goldendoodle Grooming.
<http://www.goldendoodlegrooming.com/groom-goldendoodle-home/>

"How to Potty Train a Puppy, A Comprehensive Guide for Success." Mara Bovsun. <http://www.akc.org/content/dog-training/articles/how-to-potty-train-a-puppy/>

"How to Select a Good Puppy." Dr. Ian Dunbar. <http://www.dogstardaily.com/training/how-select-good-puppy>

"Hybrid vigour...fact or fiction?" Pedigree Dogs Exposed. <http://pedigreedogsexposed.blogspot.com/2011/01/hybrid-vigour-fact-or-fiction.html>

"Hypothyroidism in Dogs." Doctors Foster and Smith. <http://www.drsfostersmith.com/pic/article.cfm?aid=1409>

"Juvenile Cataracts." Dog Channel. <http://www.dogchannel.com/dog-vet-library/eareye/article_3761.aspx>

"Juvenile Cataracts." Dr. Lisa Radosta. <http://www.petmd.com/blogs/purelypuppy/lradosta/2012/aug/juvenile_cataracts_puppy-26754>

"Kneecap Dislocation in Dogs." PetMD. <http://www.petmd.com/dog/conditions/musculoskeletal/c_multi_patellar_luxation>

"Luxating Patella." Race Foster, DVM. <http://www.peteducation.com/article.cfm?c=2+2084&aid=457>

"Off to the right start: Puppies and the critical period of socialization." Animal Humane Society.

<https://www.animalhumanesociety.org/training/right-start-socializing-your-puppy>

"Pregnancy Diagnosis & Caring for the Pregnant Dog." Pet Education. <http://www.peteducation.com/article.cfm?c=2+2109&aid=900>

"Progressive Retinal Atrophy." Eye Care for Animals. <http://www.eyecareforanimals.com/conditions/progressive-retinal-atrophy/>

"Progressive Retinal Atrophy/Degeneration in Dogs." Marty Smith, DVM. <http://www.peteducation.com/article.cfm?c=2+2092&aid=343>

"Puppy Proofing Your Home." Katherine Hillestad, DVM. <http://www.peteducation.com/article.cfm?c=2+2106&aid=3283>

"Puppy-Proofing Your Home." PetSmart. <http://pets.petsmart.com/content/new-pet/dog/puppy-proofing-your-home.shtml>

"Responsible Breeding." AKC. <http://www.akc.org/dog-breeders/responsible-breeding/>

"Retinal Dysplasia." Dogtime.com. <http://dogtime.com/definition/retinal-dysplasia>

"Retinal Dysplasia in Dogs." Pets4Homes. <http://www.pets4homes.co.uk/pet-advice/retinal-dysplasia-in-dogs.html>

"Roll with it, baby; a look at entropion and ectropion." Dr. Kim Smyth. <http://www.gopetplan.com/blogpost/roll-with-it-baby>

"Sebaceous Adenitis in Dogs." VetStreet. <http://www.vetstreet.com/care/sebaceous-adenitis-in-dogs>

"Stages of Dog Pregnancy." Kelly Roper. <http://dogs.lovetoknow.com/wiki/Dog_Pregnancy#fDg2qZckjbCIPuhd.97>

"Sudden Behavioral Changes in Your Doodle? It could be a Thyroid Issue." Jacquie York. <http://doodlerescue.org/forum/topics/sudden-behavioral-changes-in-your-doodle-it-could-be-a-thyroid-is>

"The Cost of Owning a Dog." RaisingSpot.com. <http://www.raisingspot.com/adopting/cost-of-owning-dog>

"The do's and don'ts of positive reinforcement." Josh Weiss-Roessler. <https://www.cesarsway.com/dog-training/choosing-a-professional-trainer/the-dos-and-donts-of-positive-reinforcement>

"Vaccinating Your Pet." American Humane Association. <http://www.americanhumane.org/animals/adoption-pet-care/caring-for-your-pet/vaccinating-your-pet.html>

"Vaccination Schedules for Dogs and Puppies." Pet Education. <http://www.peteducation.com/article.cfm?c=2+2115&aid=950>

"Von Willebrand's Disease in Dogs." VCA. <http://www.vcahospitals.com/main/pet-health-information/article/animal-health/von-willebrands-disease-in-dogs/872>

"What are the pros and cons of a goldendoodle?" Dogster. <http://www.dogster.com/answers/question/what_are_the_pros_and_cons_of_a_goldendoodle-35280>

"What Pet Food Makers DON'T Want You to Know." Healthy Pets. <http://healthypets.mercola.com/sites/healthypets/archive/2010/10/21/selecting-the-best-cat-pet-and-dog-pet-food.aspx>

"Where did the Goldendoodle come from?" Goldendoodles of Bar C Kennels. <http://www.barckennels.com/History.html>

"Why Should I Train My Dog?" Victoria Stilwell. <https://positively.com/dog-training/find-a-trainer/why-should-i-train-my-dog/>

"Why Train Your Dog?" American Dog Trainers Network. <http://inch.com/~dogs/whytrain.html>

Feeding Baby
Cynthia Cherry
978-1941070000

Axolotl
Lolly Brown
978-0989658430

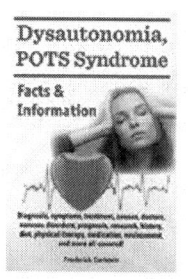

Dysautonomia, POTS Syndrome
Frederick Earlstein
978-0989658485

Degenerative Disc Disease Explained
Frederick Earlstein
978-0989658485

Sinusitis, Hay Fever,
Allergic Rhinitis Explained
Frederick Earlstein
978-1941070024

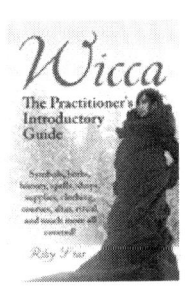

Wicca
Riley Star
978-1941070130

Zombie Apocalypse
Rex Cutty
978-1941070154

Capybara
Lolly Brown
978-1941070062

Eels As Pets
Lolly Brown
978-1941070167

Scabies and Lice Explained
Frederick Earlstein
978-1941070017

Saltwater Fish As Pets
Lolly Brown
978-0989658461

Torticollis Explained
Frederick Earlstein
978-1941070055

Kennel Cough
Lolly Brown
978-0989658409

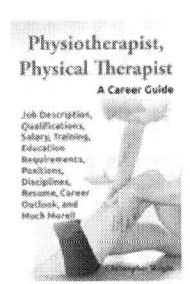

Physiotherapist, Physical Therapist
Christopher Wright
978-0989658492

Rats, Mice, and Dormice As Pets
Lolly Brown
978-1941070079

Wallaby and Wallaroo Care
Lolly Brown
978-1941070031

Bodybuilding Supplements Explained
Jon Shelton
978-1941070239

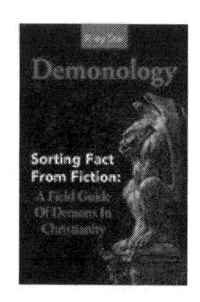

Demonology
Riley Star
978-19401070314

Pigeon Racing
Lolly Brown
978-1941070307

Dwarf Hamster
Lolly Brown
978-1941070390

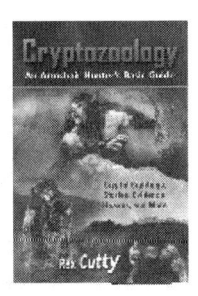

Cryptozoology
Rex Cutty
978-1941070406

Eye Strain
Frederick Earlstein
978-1941070369

Inez The Miniature Elephant
Asher Ray
978-1941070353

Vampire Apocalypse
Rex Cutty
978-1941070321

Made in the USA
Lexington, KY
28 August 2019